Esposito Javet

67   De aedibus

Esposito Javet

Quart Verlag Luzern

Esposito Javet
67. Band der Reihe De aedibus / Volume 67 of the series De aedibus

Herausgeber / Edited by: Heinz Wirz, Luzern
Konzept / Concept: Heinz Wirz; Esposito Javet, Lausanne
Projektleitung / Project management: Quart Verlag, Linus Wirz
Textbeitrag / Article by: Paul Chemetov, Paris
Projekttexte / Project descriptions: Esposito Javet
Vorwort / Foreword: Heinz Wirz
Textlektorat Deutsch / German text editing: Miriam Seifert-Waibel, Hamburg
Textlektorat Englisch / English text editing: Benjamin Liebelt, Berlin
Übersetzung Französisch–Deutsch / French–German translation: Christian Rochow, Berlin
Übersetzung Französisch–Englisch / French–English translation: John Baker, Neschers F
Übersetzung Deutsch–Englisch / German–English translation:
Benjamin Liebelt S./p. 7 (Notat)
Fotos / Photos: Thomas Jantscher, Milvignes; ausser/except: Matthieu Gafsou, Pully S./p. 73, 74, 89, 91–93, 96; Esposito Javet S./p. 94, 95; Alfonso Esposito S./p. 36
Grafische Umsetzung / Graphic design: Quart Verlag
Lithos: Printeria, Luzern
Druck / Printing: DZA Druckerei zu Altenburg GmbH

© Copyright 2017
Quart Verlag Luzern, Heinz Wirz
Alle Rechte vorbehalten / All rights reserved
ISBN 978-3-03761-144-9

Egalement publié en allemand/français / Ebenfalls publiziert
in Deutsch/Französisch (ISBN 978-3-03761-165-4)

Quart Verlag GmbH
Denkmalstrasse 2, CH-6006 Luzern
books@quart.ch, www.quart.ch

7	De aedibus 67 – Notat Heinz Wirz
8	Die Raffinesse der einfachen Wörter / The sophistication of simple words Paul Chemetov, Paris
12	Arnon-Schule / Arnon School, Fiez
18	Schulzentrum / School centre, Vers-chez-les-Blanc
24	Schulzentrum Léman / Léman school centre, Renens
32	Flugzeugwaschhalle / Washing bay, Payerne
38	Studentenwohnheime / Student accommodation, Saint-Sulpice
42	Wohn- und Pflegeheim Bois-Gentil / Bois-Gentil residential and nursing home, Lausanne
48	Wohn- und Pflegeheim Le Marronnier / Le Marronnier residential and nursing home, Lutry
54	Gemeindehaus / Municipal building, Chavannes-des-Bois
60	Wohn- und Pflegeheim Pré-Fleuri / Pré-Fleuri residential and nursing home, Lausanne
64	Censuy-Schule / Censuy School, Renens
70	Stadtvilla Chailly / Chailly urban villa, Lausanne
76	Schulzentrum Mabillon / Mabillon school centre, Monthey
82	Veranstaltungssaal der *Usine à Gaz* und Wohngebäude / Event hall for the *Usine à Gaz* and housing development, Nyon
88	Wohn- und Pflegeheim Les Fauvettes / Les Fauvettes residential and nursing home, Montagny-la-Ville
94	Werkverzeichnis / List of works
96	Biografien, Auszeichnungen, Ausstellungen, Bibliografie Biographies, Awards, Exhibitions, Bibliography

De aedibus 67 – Notat
Heinz Wirz

Alfonso Esposito und Anne-Catherine Javet sind beide in der Westschweiz geboren, aufgewachsen und an der EPF Lausanne haben sie ihre Studien absolviert. Als Studenten und Assistenten von Luigi Snozzi, dem vielleicht einflussreichsten Protagonisten und Wortführer der Tessiner «Tendenza», lernten sie wichtige Parameter der Architektur kennen: die Bedeutung des Orts, der Topografie, das Erbe der Moderne, starke Formen und klare kubische Baukörper. Sie waren von Luigi Snozzi wie Axiome gesetzt.

Und trotzdem, ihr erstes Werk – nach sechs gewonnenen Wettbewerben –, die Arnon-Schule in Fiez, entsprach – zumindest in ihrem Äussern – ganz und gar nicht diesen Vorstellungen. Das ganz in Holz gekleidete Gebäude, mitten in einem weitläufigen Wiesenfeld, gemahnt an eine grosse Scheune. Es entspricht dem klaren architektonischen Willen, die Funktion in eine Form zu binden, die sich mit den archaischen Formen der ruralen Architektur des Orts verbindet. Diese starke, bewusste Geste der Integration erinnert spontan an das Théâtre du Jorat aus dem Jahr 1908 in Mézières, das die Funktion des Theaters nicht in eine noble, klassizistische Architektur kleidet, sondern das rurale Pendant dazu bevorzugt. Diese architektonische Grundhaltung verfolgen die Architekten bei weiteren Bauten in ländlicher Umgebung. Das Äussere, sozusagen das Gewand, entspricht im besten Sinne der Stimmung des Orts und seiner Umgebung. Das Innere hingegen wendet sich gleichsam dem zeitgenössischen Leben zu und entfaltet dabei höchste räumliche und architektonische Qualitäten in der Sprache der Moderne. Beim Gemeindehaus von Chavannes-des-Bois werden die grosse Eingangshalle, das Treppenhaus und die Erschliessungsgänge zu einladenden, feierlichen, differenzierten Innenraumfiguren. Diese und die klare, und übersichtliche Grundrissstruktur entsprechen so ganz dem mies-van-der-roheschen «Interesse für Würde und Wert» und der Vorstellung von «organischem Ordnungsprinzip».

Diese Qualitäten führen wie ein roter Faden durch alle Projekte von Esposito und Javet. Und schliesslich finden wir bei den Setzungen der Bauten zu Ensembles untereinander und in der Bezugnahme zu bestehenden Bauten und Siedlungen eine auffällige Sorgfalt und Integration. Dies geschieht mit einer Selbstverständlichkeit und Gelassenheit, was uns gleichsam wieder zurückführt zum Erbe von Luigi Snozzi.

Luzern, im September 2017

De aedibus 67 – Notat
Heinz Wirz

Alfonso Esposito and Anne-Catherine Javet were both born in western Switzerland and graduated here at the EPF Lausanne. As students of and Assistants to Luigi Snozzi, who is perhaps the most influential protagonist and spokesman of the Ticino "Tendenza", they encountered important parameters of architecture: the significance of the location, topography, modern heritage, powerful forms and clear, cuboid volumes, all of which were defined as axioms by Luigi Snozzi.

Nevertheless after winning six competitions, their first work, the Arnon School in Fiez, did not at all conform to those principles – at least in terms of its exterior. The building, which is completely clad in wood, is situated in the middle of an expansive meadow and recalls a large barn. It reflects the clear architectural will to bind the function into a form that connects with the archaic forms of the local rural architecture. This powerful, conscious gesture of integration inspires spontaneous comparison with the 1908 Théâtre du Jorat in Mézières, which also prefers a rural equivalent rather than cladding the function of the theatre in noble, neo-classical architecture. The architects reveal the same underlying architectural approach in other buildings in rural surroundings. The vesture-like exterior conforms to the atmosphere of the location and its surroundings in the best sense of the word. By contrast, the interior is dedicated to contemporary life, thereby developing the highest spatial and architectural qualities in a modern language. In the case of the Chavannes-des-Bois community hall, the large entrance area, the staircase and the connecting corridors become inviting, festive, distinct interior spatial figures. These characteristics and the clear, concisely structured floor plan correspond to Mies van der Rohe's interest in "dignity and value", as well as his perception of an "organic principle of order". Such qualities run like a thread through all projects by Esposito and Javet. Finally, their care and integrative stance is apparent in the way the buildings are placed to form ensembles and also in their references to existing buildings and estates. In doing so, they express a matter-of-factness that reflects the legacy of Luigi Snozzi.

Lucerne, September 2017

Die Raffinesse der einfachen Wörter

Paul Chemetov

Um das gemeinsame Werk von Anne-Catherine Javet und Alfonso Esposito besser betrachten und verstehen zu können, muss ich zunächst über ihre Lebensläufe und ihren beruflichen Werdegang sprechen.

Die beiden Architekten wurden im selben Jahr geboren und erwarben auch im selben Jahr ihr Architekturdiplom bei Luigi Snozzi an der Ecole Polytechnique Fédérale de Lausanne (EPFL). Man weiss um den grossen und bleibenden Einfluss dieses einzigartigen, radikalen, im dostojewskis'schen Sinne grossinquisitorischen Mannes – eines Treibenden und Getriebenen – auf seine Zeit, seine Schüler und seine Berufskollegen. Paukenschlägen gleich garnierte er seine Lehre mit einigen beispielhaften Bauten in dem kleinen Dorf Monte Carasso.

Wenn beide, nach Stationen bei Purini beziehungsweise bei Cruz und Ortiz, ihre beruflichen Grundlagen in der Schweiz erlernten, dann vor allem im Büro von Snozzi, wo Anne-Catherine arbeitete. Beide waren Assistenten an der EPFL, Anne-Catherine bei Luigi Snozzi und Alfonso bei vier Gastprofessoren, von denen ich einer war. Aber es war Snozzi, der bei einer Besichtigung der Léman-Schule erklärte: «Ich glaubte nicht, dass Sie in der Lage sind, ein solches Gebäude zu realisieren.»

Nach mehreren Jahren der Selbstständigkeit gründeten sie im Jahr 2003 ihr gemeinsames Büro. Es sind also die Arbeiten dieser ersten Jahre, die in diesem Buch vorgestellt werden: Rund 50 Projekte und ein Dutzend realisierter Bauten kommen hier zusammen.

Die Architektur ist ein Metier des Reifens, der Erfahrung. Man muss stets auf das erste Werk zurückkommen, weil es verrät, was bewusst und unbewusst schon da ist in der Arbeit jedes Architekten. Auf gewisse Art zeigt das Werk seinen Urheber und enthüllt etwas Uraltes, vielleicht sogar Archaisches. «Gründlich», sagt man auf Deutsch. Dafür gibt es kein französisches Äquivalent. Es handelt sich um ein fundamentales Sich-auf-den-Boden-Stützen.

Die Arnon-Schule könnte eine Scheune sein, aber eine übersteigerte, raffinierte Version. Das fast quadratische Gebäude wirkt auf den ersten Blick lakonisch, will aber genau analysiert sein, denn es wird von harmonischen Linienführungen bestimmt und gegliedert, die für jene erkennbar sind, die sie zu lesen verstehen. Im Erscheinungsbild erkennt man zwei gleichförmige Streifen, den der bedienten und den der dienenden Flächen, die die sanitären Anlagen und die Treppe aufnehmen. Das ist bereits der Prototyp aller künftigen Arbeiten. Betonte Geländer, verfeinert durch das Herausarbeiten des Handlaufs – diese Verfeinerung setzt sich

The sophistication of simple words

Paul Chemetov

To enable the reader to better visualise and understand the joint work of Anne-Catherine Javet and Alfonso Eposito, I must first talk about them, their education and their lives.

Born in the same year, they also graduated the same year from the EPFL under the aegis of Luigi Snozzi. We are fully aware of the influence of this singular, radical man, the Grand Inquisitor in the Dostoyevskian sense of the word, the persecuted persecutor, whose influence on his students, his colleagues and his era was and still is considerable. He punctuated his teaching with a number of iconic edifices in a small town, Monte Carasso, like so many tolls of a bell.

While they both gained practical experience in Switzerland after placements with Purini and with Cruz and Ortiz, Anne-Catherine worked in Snozzi's studio. They were both Assistants at the EPFL, Anne-Catherine to Luigi Snozzi and Alfonso to four Guest Professors, including myself. But it was Snozzi who, visiting the Ecole du Léman, stated, "I didn't think you were capable of creating such a building."

After a few years working independently, they set up their joint office in 2003. This publication brings together the works of these early years, including some fifty projects and a dozen completed buildings.

Architecture is a profession in which we mature and gain experience, but you must always return to the first work that reveals what was already there, both consciously and subconsciously, in the work of any architect. To a certain extent, the work identifies the author and reveals something atavistic, perhaps even archaic. "Gründlich" as the Germans might say. The word has no equivalent in English and means fundamental and building from the ground up.

The Arnon School could be a barn, albeit an exaggerated, sophisticated one. At first glance it is laconic, but it is necessary to dissect this almost-square, governed and divided by harmonic almost-alignments, which are clear to those who know how to read them. There seem to be two equal bands: the space that is served and the space that serves, housing the toilets and the stairs. This is the prototype of what was to follow. Pronounced banisters, refined by the marking of the handrail, a refinement reflected in the glazed guardrails of the municipal building in Chavannes-des-Bois and stair stringers at the Bois-Gentil residential and nursing home. The staircase is enhanced by the scattered light and the feeling of unity created by the ubiquitous colour green. This staircase presages those of the Vers-chez-les-Blanc and Censuy schools.

fort in den Glasgeländern des Gemeindehauses von Chavannes-des-Bois, in den Treppenwangen des Wohn- und Pflegeheims Bois-Gentil. Das Treppenhaus wird autonom durch die Lichtführung und die einheitliche grüne Farbe. Diese Treppe weist voraus auf jene des Schulzentrums Vers-chez-les-Blanc und der Censuy-Schule.

Die Aussenverkleidung der Arnon-Schule ist mit Abdeckleisten versehen, die sich vor den Fensteröffnungen zugleich als Gitter und als Sonnenblende fortsetzen. Das ist der Nullpunkt der Formensprache, aber tatsächlich ist damit alles gesagt. Man kann dieses Thema in den Blechplatten zur Verkleidung des Gemeindehauses von Chavannes-des-Bois wiederfinden. Geht nicht jeder Architekt über seine Bezüge hinaus – die im Gefüge des Werks unverzichtbar sind – hartnäckig bestimmten materiellen Themen nach, die ihm wesentlich sind, indem er sie deformiert, sie übernimmt, bei jeder Gelegenheit über sie stolpert? Ist das Zufall oder Notwendigkeit? Oder vielleicht Zufall und Notwendigkeit?

So lässt sich das quadratische Prinzip der Arnon-Schule in Fiez in dem perfekten Quadrat und genauso in der harmonischen Linienführung des Wohn- und Pflegeheims Pré-Fleuri wiederfinden. Aber in einer unausgesetzten Bewegung verformt sich die orthogonale Geometrie manchmal, um auf die Präsenz eines bestehenden Gebäudes zu reagieren, das in das praktische und ästhetische Funktionieren des Gesamten integriert werden muss, und das geschieht manchmal selbsttätig wie beim Projekt des Schulzentrums in Monthey oder beim Projekt des Wohn- und Pflegeheims in Montagny-la-Ville – Letzteres zeigt den Gegensatz zwischen einer Figur, die im Grundriss komplex und im Aufriss orthogonal ist, und einem Gebäude, das in seinem Grundriss orthogonal und in seinem Aufriss uneinheitlich ist.

Das Schulzetrum Léman in Renens erscheint mir als der Abschluss und das Resümee dieser Serie. Esposito und Javet weisen Snozzis Aussage zurück: Sie waren fähig, dieses Projekt zu vollenden, weil es die Verlängerung dessen ist, was sie ursprünglich und natürlich seit ihrem ersten Werk ausgesagt haben.

Im Grundriss werden Spannweiten und Zäsuren rund um einen zentralen Leerraum in der dynamischen Verteilung der Trennwände in Bewegung gebracht; hinzu kommt das grosse konstruktive Problem einer Sporthalle, die zum Ausgleich des Bodenniveaus teilweise versenkt ist. Zur Lösung trägt das Aussenskelett aus Vierendeelträgern bei, das auch den Überhang an der Ecke ermöglicht, der den Eingang kennzeichnet.

Wer es sehen will, kann hier die Logik italienischer Palazzi mit Hof wiederfinden und vielleicht auch eine unbewusste Erinnerung an das Œuvre von Marc Camoletti, das ein Forschungsgegenstand an der EPFL war.

The exterior cladding of the Arnon School is ribbed with joint covers which extend in front of the bay windows, serving both as a grille and a sunshade. This is the starting point, but it already says all there is to say. The theme can be seen in the cladding sheets of the municipal building in Chavannes-des-Bois. Beyond their own references, primordial in creating edifices, does not every architect obstinately pursue certain material themes essential to them, distorting and adopting them, sometimes stumbling on each circumstance? Chance or necessity? Chance and necessity?

Accordingly, the square principle in Fiez can be found in the perfect square and the equally clear harmonic lines of the Pré-Fleuri residence. Yet in a continuous movement, the orthogonal geometry is sometimes distorted in response to the presence of an existing building which must be incorporated into the practical and aesthetic workings of the whole, or is sometimes self-generated as in the Monthey school group project or in the Montagny-la-Ville residential and nursing home project – the most recent to be documented – in which a figure with a geometrically complex plan and orthogonal elevations contrasts with a construction displaying an orthogonal plan and eclectic elevations.

The Léman school centre in Renens seems to me to be the culmination and synopsis of this series. Let us repay his compliment to Snozzi. Esposito and Javet were capable of completing this project because it is the extension of what they initially and naturally expressed from their very first work.

On the plan, it is the movement of the spans and breaks around an empty central area in the dynamic distribution of the partition walls, combined with the major structural difficulty of a gymnasium, partly excavated in the differing ground level. The Vierendeel beam outer frame contributes to this, facilitating the corner cantilever indicating the entrance.

Anyone willing to see it can discern the rationale of Italian palaces with a courtyard, and perhaps even the subconscious memory of Camoletti's work, which was a theme at the EPFL.

However, what I see as symptomatic of this project and its intentions is the transformation of the existing building so that it reflects the atmosphere and rationality of the new building, while a third building remains in its former state – further work for the coming years.

It was noted that in all these cases of confrontation, Esposito and Javet never chose the road of mimicry, and yet the contemporary radicalism of their buildings clearly goes hand in hand with past architectures, weighed down with too many references.

We could discuss the deformation of the original square or the influence of the contemporary design forms, while observing that from the Saint-Sulpice

Was mir aber an diesem Projekt und seinen Absichten als symptomatisch erscheint, ist die Transformation des bestehenden Gebäudes, damit es in Atmosphäre und Rationalität mit dem neuen übereinstimmt. Es bleibt noch ein drittes in altem Zustand. Dies wird eine Arbeit der kommenden Jahre sein.
Es ist festzuhalten, dass sich in allen diesen Fällen einer Konfrontation Esposito und Javet niemals auf die Seite einer nachahmenden Mimikry schlugen. Dennoch passt die zeitgenössische Radikalität ihrer Gebäude deutlich zu den Architekturen der Vergangenheit, die von einem Gewicht zu vieler Bezüge belastet sind.
Man könnte über die Verformung des gründenden Quadrats oder über den Einfluss der Formen des zeitgenössischen Designs Bemerkungen machen, aber genauso gut feststellen, dass sich seit den Studentenwohnheimen in Saint-Sulpice der rechte Winkel als Notwendigkeit bei der Erschliessung oder als höfliche Geste gegenüber dem Bestandsgebäude des Wohn- und Pflegeheims in Lutry durchsetzt. Die Frage, die sich jeder Architekt stellen muss und der auch Esposito und Javet begegnen, ist die der Unregelmässigkeit. Man kann aus dem Natürlichen keinen französischen Garten gewinnen, aber man kann und muss die Linien eines französischen Gartens mit den als natürlich empfundenen eines englischen Landschaftsparks kombinieren, der das herausarbeitet, was in den Zügen der Landschaft bereits vorfindlich ist. Niemals aber erscheinen im Werk von Esposito und Javet jene Marotten, die heute in der architektonischen Bildwelt so weitverbreitet sind: frei geformte Flächen, die an die Formen von Tarnkappenflugzeugen erinnern, oder Aussenverkleidungen, die ausschauen wie Tapeten. Die Flugzeugwaschhalle ist ein schönes Beispiel: Ihr Lowtech- oder, wenn man will, Alltagstechansatz charakterisiert alle Arbeiten von Esposito und Javet. Liegt hier vielleicht ein schweizerischer Fundamentalismus vor? Ein französischer Beobachter könnte diesen beispielsweise im Raffinement des (scheinbar) einfachen Worts bei Charles-Ferdinand Ramuz entdecken oder auch in der leichten Satzmelodie des schweizerischen Französisch.
Wie lassen sich lokal und global vereinbaren? Kenneth Frampton stellte schon diese Frage, die angesichts des anonymen, gemeinsam genutzten und heute computergenerierten Charakters des Neo-International Style eine wesentliche ist. Gerade auch deswegen sollten wir den erdverbundenen, weil umsichtig mit dem jeweiligen Gelände umgehenden Charakter der Bauten von Esposito Javet schätzen. Und da die beiden Architekten gerade erst ihr 50. Lebensjahr überschritten und damit wie alle Architekten die Reifezeit ihres Schaffen erreicht haben, sollten wir mit Geduld und Freude die weitere Entwicklung ihres Œuvres verfolgen.

Paris, im Januar 2017

student accommodation, angulation becomes necessary for distribution, or as a courtesy to the existing building at the residential and nursing home in Lutry. The question that every architect has to deal with, and that Esposito and Javet have also encountered, is that of irregularity. We cannot transform nature into a French garden, but we can and must combine the lines of a French garden with the natural feel of the lines of an English garden, emphasising what already exists in the ever-moving landscape. However, the works of Esposito and Javet never display the quirks that have become so widespread in architectural imagery: awkward areas reminiscent of stealth aircraft and cladding recalling wallpaper. The washing area is a perfect example of this: its low-tech, or might we even say common-tech, approach is characteristic of all the work produced by Esposito and Javet. Could this be redolent of Swiss fundamentalism? A French observer might find it in the refinement of the – seemingly simple words of CF Ramuz, while sensing the slight intonation given to the French pronunciation in Switzerland.
How can we be local in a global world? Kenneth Frampton saw this as an essential question in light of the anonymity, shared and now digitised, of the international neo-style. Let us taste and appreciate the earthy flavour – attentive to the different sites – of the work of Esposito Javet. And now that they have celebrated their fiftieth birthdays, the age of maturity of every architect, let us patiently await, our mouths watering, their work still to come.

Paris, January 2017

Arnon-Schule, Fiez

Arnon School, Fiez

Das Programm des Architekturwettbewerbs sah eine Sporthalle und ein Schulgebäude mit sechs Klassenzimmern und weiteren Einrichtungen (Bibliothek, Lehrerzimmer, Sanitätsstation) vor. Bislang wurde nur das Schulgebäude realisiert. Es steht auf dem ebensten Teil des Grundstücks und grenzt im Westen den Schulhof ab, der eine Verbindung zu der durch das Dorf führenden Strasse herstellt. Die Sporthalle am Hang würde den Schulhof nach Norden abschliessen. Die Neigung des Geländes wird dazu genutzt, einen Teil des Programms unter die Erde zu verlegen, um das auf dem Gelände sichtbare Volumen zu verkleinern.

Die Realisierung dieser aus Holz errichteten Schule gibt sich schlicht und bescheiden – im Einklang mit den Scheunen und landwirtschaftlichen Gebäuden in der Nachbarschaft. Die Abdeckleisten, die zwischen den Holzpaneelen der Fassadenverkleidung angebracht sind, erzeugen ein Licht-und-Schatten-Spiel, das der Fassade Tiefe und eine besondere Oberflächenstruktur verleiht; vor den grossen Fensteröffnungen der Klassenzimmer verwandeln sie sich in eine Art Lattenzaun.

The architectural design competition stipulated the construction of a sports hall and a school with 6 classrooms and accompanying facilities (library, staffroom and infirmary). At present, only the school building has been completed. Built on the flattest section of the plot of land, it demarcates the school yard to the west which links to the road through the village. The sports hall will form the northern edge of the yard while incorporating part of the building into the slope in order to reduce its visual presence on the site.

This wooden school building is designed to be simple and modest, reflecting the barns and other farm buildings in the surrounding area. The joint covers placed between the wooden slats of the exterior cladding create a light and shadow effect, lending the façade a thickness and specific texture while taking the form of louvres in front of the bay windows of the classrooms.

Wettbewerb / Competition: 2004
Ausführung / Construction: 2006–2007
Bauherrschaft / Client: Gemeinde Fiez / Municipality of Fiez
Mitarbeit / Collaborators: Omar Trinca, Vincent Roesti, Nicolas Meyer
Bauleitung / Construction management: R. Delaporte
Bauingenieur / Structural engineer: Perret Gentil SA
Elektroplanung / Electrical planning: Perrin & Spaeth SA
Heizungs-, Lüftungs- und Sanitärplanung / Heating, ventilation and sanitary planner: AZ Ingénieurs SA

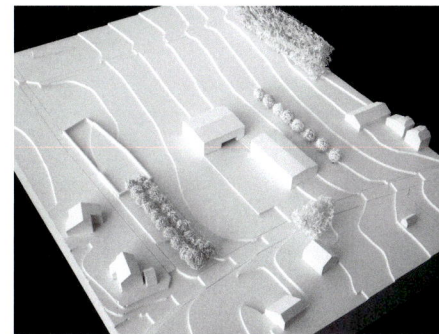

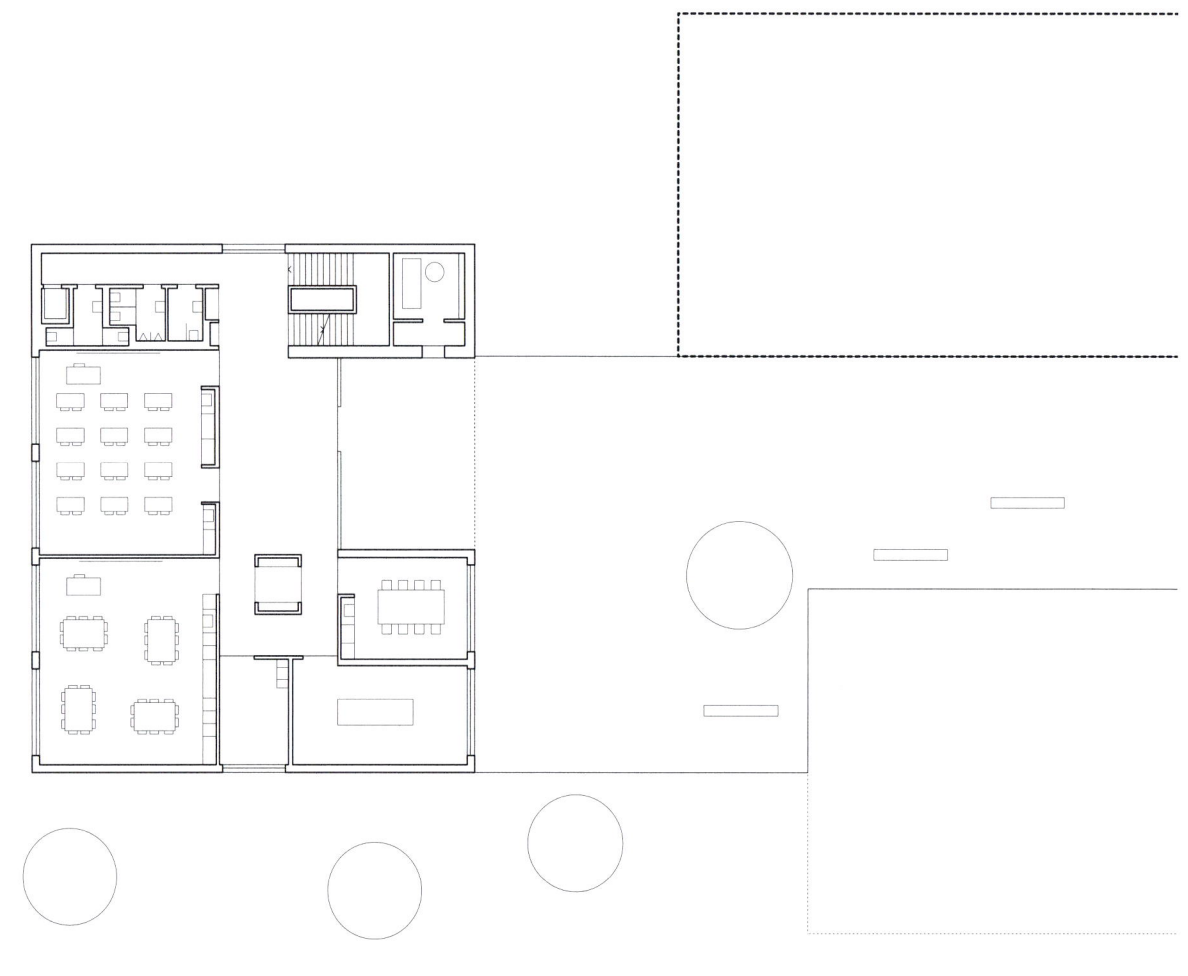

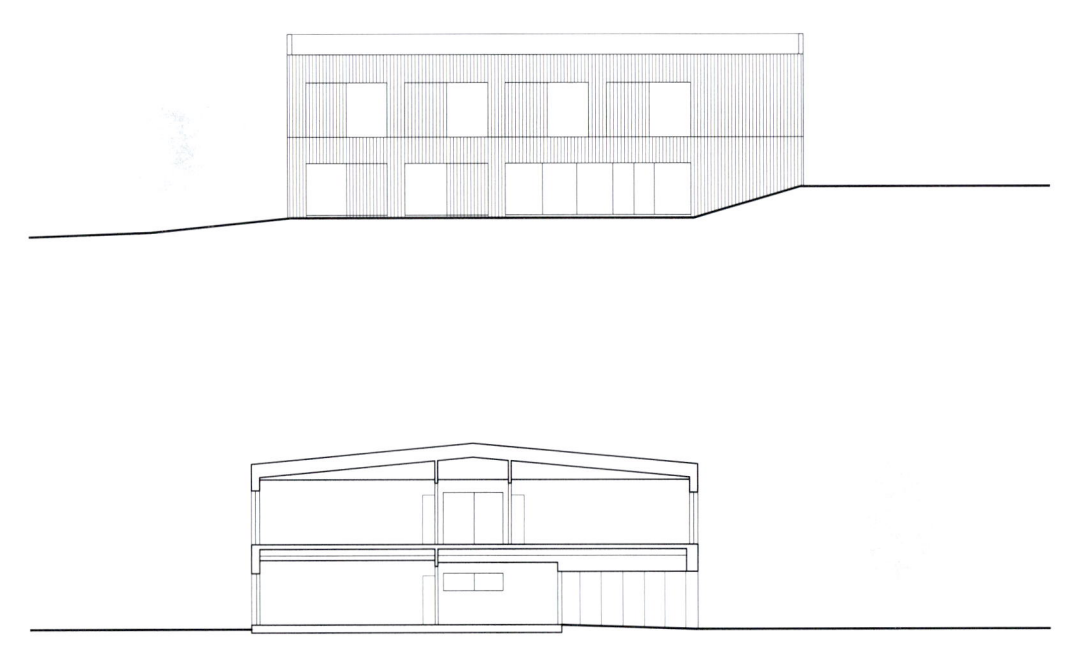

Schulzentrum, Vers-chez-les-Blanc

School centre, Vers-chez-les-Blanc

In einer zersiedelten Gemeinde, die durch das Fehlen eines öffentlichen Raums, der als Bezugspunkt dienen könnte, charakterisiert war, bot die Erweiterung des Schulzentrums die Gelegenheit, einen Treffpunkt für die Einwohner des Orts zu schaffen. Versetzt zu den Bestandsgebäuden angeordnet wahrt das neue Ensemble der Schule die Autonomie der einzelnen Bauten und erzeugt eine Abfolge charakteristischer Höfe mit unterschiedlichen Stimmungen, die dem Gelände folgend stufenförmig angeordnet sind. Das Gebäude, das die neuen Klassenzimmer aufnimmt, stellt durch die unterschiedliche Orientierung der Verkehrsflächen und Klassenzimmer, die zur umliegenden Landschaft ausgerichtet sind, einen Bezug zu allen diesen Höfen her.

Die bewusst zurückgenommene Volumetrie des neuen Gebäudes wahrt die Höhe der Simskante des bestehenden Schulgebäudes und passt sich so dem bescheidenen Massstab der Gebäude des Dorfs an, nimmt aber dennoch die vorgesehenen Klassenzimmer auf, die grösser sind als die in den Bestandsgebäuden.

Der Kontrast und die Nähe der drei Schulgebäude begünstigen einen Dialog zwischen Alt und Neu; auf eine nachahmende Anpassung wurde verzichtet.

In a village of scattered buildings characterised by the lack of a designated public space, the expansion of the existing school offered a pretext to create a gathering place for the local inhabitants. By not aligning with the existing buildings, the new school resulted in an entity in which the autonomy of each building was retained while creating a series of tiered courtyards up the slope, each with its own character and atmosphere.

The building housing the new classrooms is connected to each of these yards by the different orientations of the hallways and classrooms stretching out into the surrounding countryside.

By following the alignment of the cornices of the existing school buildings, the deliberately limited scale of the new construction reflects the small scale of the buildings in the village while incorporating larger classrooms than those in the existing buildings.

The offset nature and proximity of the three school buildings encourages dialogue between the old and the new while avoiding the temptation to imitate the existing structures.

Wettbewerb / Competition: 2003
Ausführung / Construction: 2006–2007
Bauherrschaft / Client: Stadt Lausanne / City of Lausanne
Mitarbeit / Collaborators: Omar Trinca, Carmen Chabloz, Mikhail Broger
Bauleitung / Construction management: J.-P. Aubert
Bauingenieur / Structural engineer: Alberti Ingénieurs SA
Bauphysik / Structural physics: Sorane SA
Elektroplanung / Electrical planning: Scherler Ingénieurs-Conseils SA
Heizungs-, Lüftungs- und Sanitärplanung / Heating, ventilation and sanitary planner: AZ Ingénieurs SA

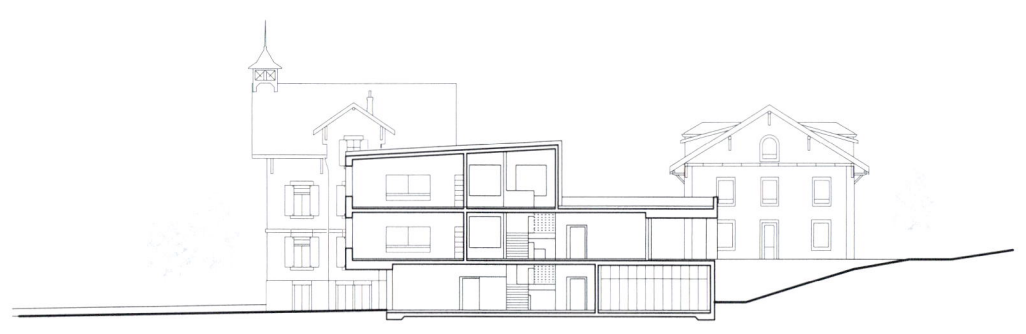

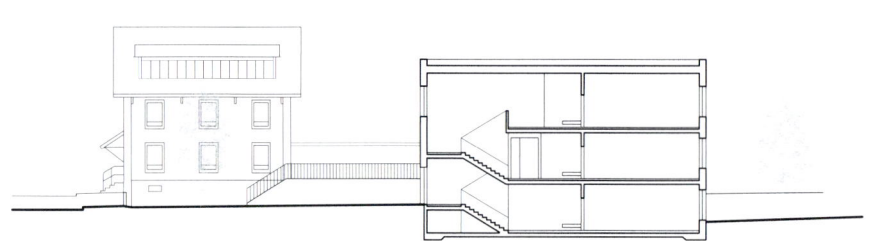

10 m

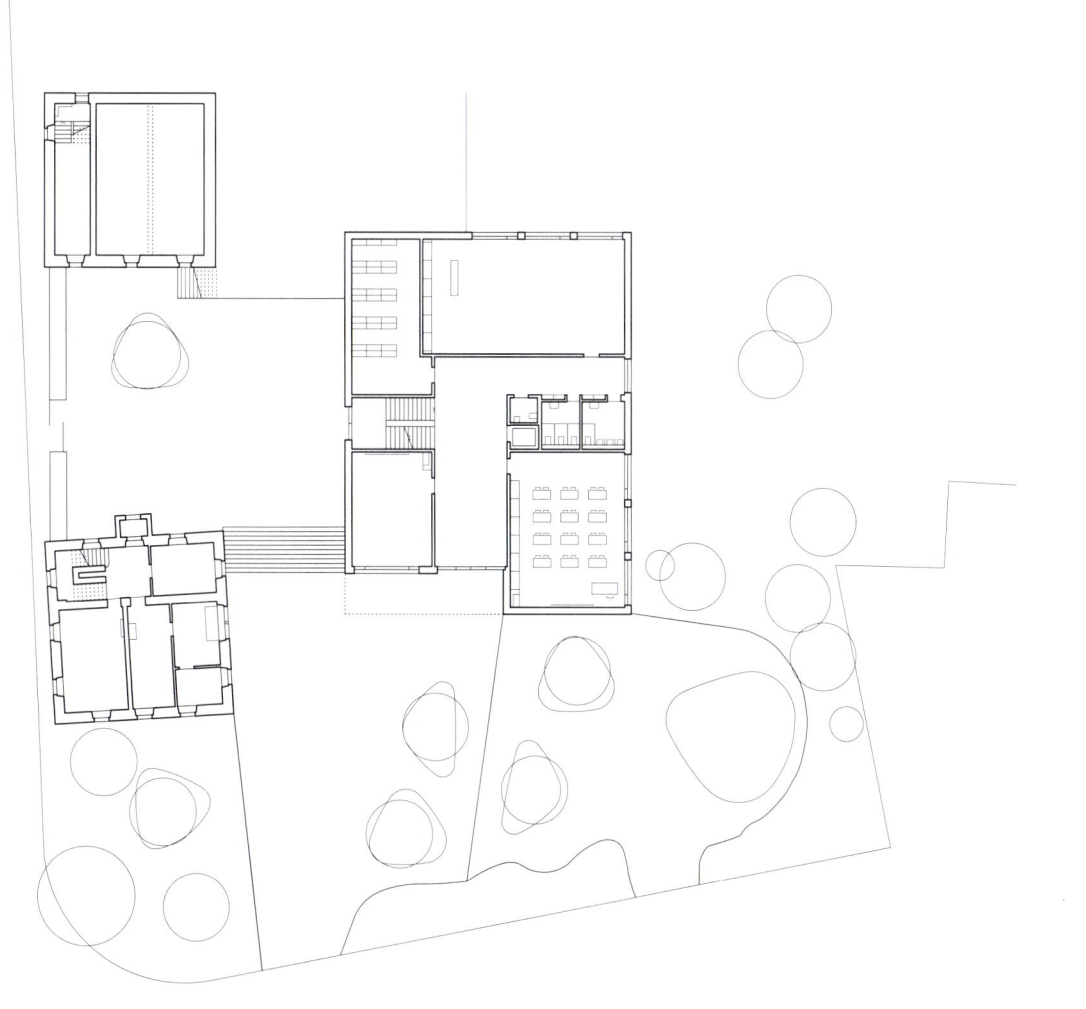

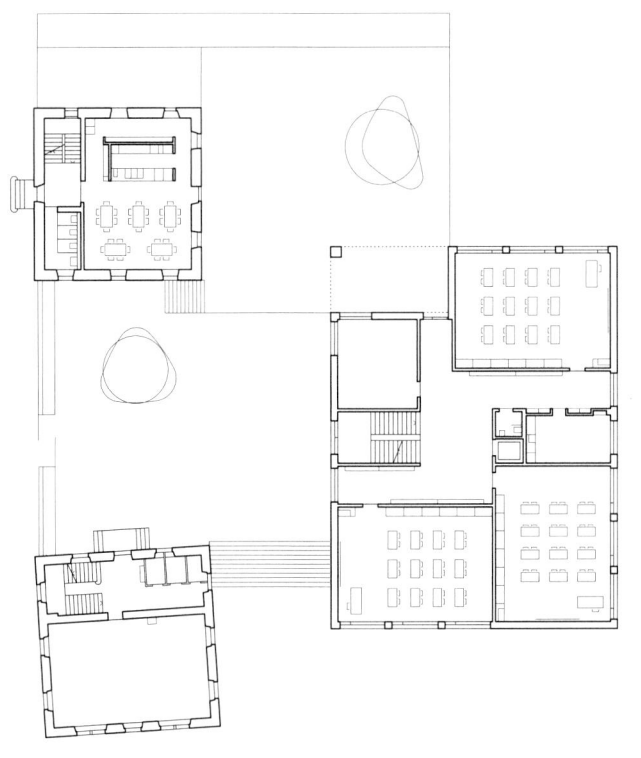

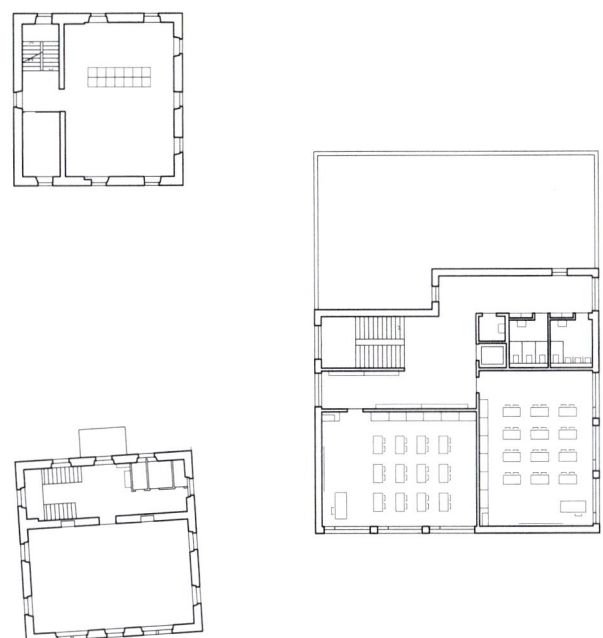

Schulzentrum Léman, Renens

Léman school centre, Renens

Die beiden auf einem grossen Parkgelände stehenden modularen Stahlbetonbauten aus den 1970er-Jahren wurden mit einem dritten Gebäude komplettiert. Das Ensemble fasst einen aufgewerteten grossen zentralen Schulhof ein. Die Gebäude und ihre äusseren Verlängerungen «durchdringen» sich von einer Seite zur anderen und schaffen Bezüge zu den verschiedenen Abschnitten des Geländes: den Sportanlagen und einem Schwimmbad im Süden und den Wohnungen rundherum. Das neue Gebäude steht am Rand der Rue du Léman auf einer geneigten Bruchkante. Die innere Verbindung zwischen der Rue du Léman und dem tiefer liegenden Schulhof über ein Lichtatrium erzeugt einen auf jeder Ebene anderen Zugang. Die typologische Konzeption stellt eine Neuinterpretation der bestehenden Schule dar, bei der die Flure und Klassenzimmer kranzförmig um einen dunklen zentralen Innenraum verteilt sind. Sie unterscheidet sich von der Vorlage durch die spiralförmige Anordnung der Flure und Klassenzimmer um ein grosses, von natürlichem Licht durchflutetes zentrales Atrium, das schöne Ausblicke von der Mitte des Gebäudes aus ermöglicht. Das komplexe und vielfältige Programm (Sporthallen, eine Mehrzweckhalle, der Speisesaal für die Schüler und Klassenzimmer) in einem einzigen Gebäude unterzubringen, war möglich dank des Rückgriffs auf ein Tragwerk aus Stahlbeton, das sich an der Fassade als ein Raster aus Vierendeelträgern und im Innern in Form von Wandscheiben zeigt, die Durchbrüche von grosser Tragweite ermöglichen.

The two, modular steel buildings dating back to the 1970s located in a large park were completed with the addition of a third building, bringing them all together around a large, redefined central courtyard. The buildings, along with their outside extensions, "cross each other" quite naturally from one end to the other, interconnecting the different sections of the site including the playing fields and a swimming pool to the south and housing areas all around. The new building is located alongside the Rue du Léman, on a break in the slope. The light atrium connecting the Rue du Léman and the school yard below provides differentiated access to each level. Its typological design is a reinterpretation of that of the existing school, the hallways and classrooms forming a crown around a dark central area. It differs from its model in the spiral organisation of the hallways and classrooms around the vast central atrium bathed in natural light, offering attractive views outside from the very heart of the building. Superimposing a complex and diversified project (sports halls, a multipurpose hall, school canteen and classrooms) in a homogenous building was made possible by creating a supporting structure in reinforced concrete showing a grid of Vierendeel beams on the outside and shear walls on the inside that support large spans.

Wettbewerb / Competition: 2005
Ausführung / Construction: 2007–2009
Bauherrschaft / Client: Stadt Renens / Municipality of Renens
Mitarbeit / Collaborators: Anne-Christine Moonen, Mikhail Broger
Bauleitung / Construction management: Regtec SA
Bauingenieur / Structural engineer: Ingeni SA & Lurati Muttoni Partner
Bauphysik / Structural physics: Sorane SA
Elektroplanung / Electrical planning: Perrottet Ingénieurs Conseil en Electricité SA
Heizungs- und Lüftungsplanung / Heating and ventilation planner: Pierre Chuard Ingénieurs Conseils SA
Sanitärplanung / Sanitary planning: Saniplans SA
Landschaftsarchitekt / Landscape architecture: Paysagestion SA
Lichtkonzept / Lighting design: Aebischer & Bovigny

25

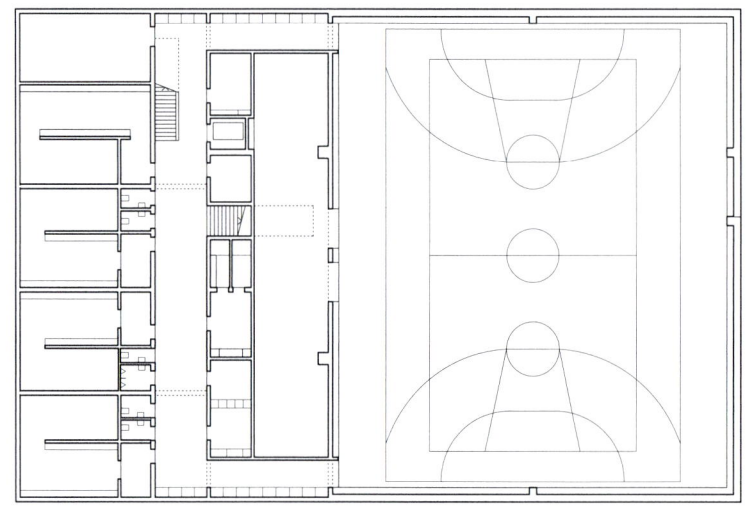

10 m

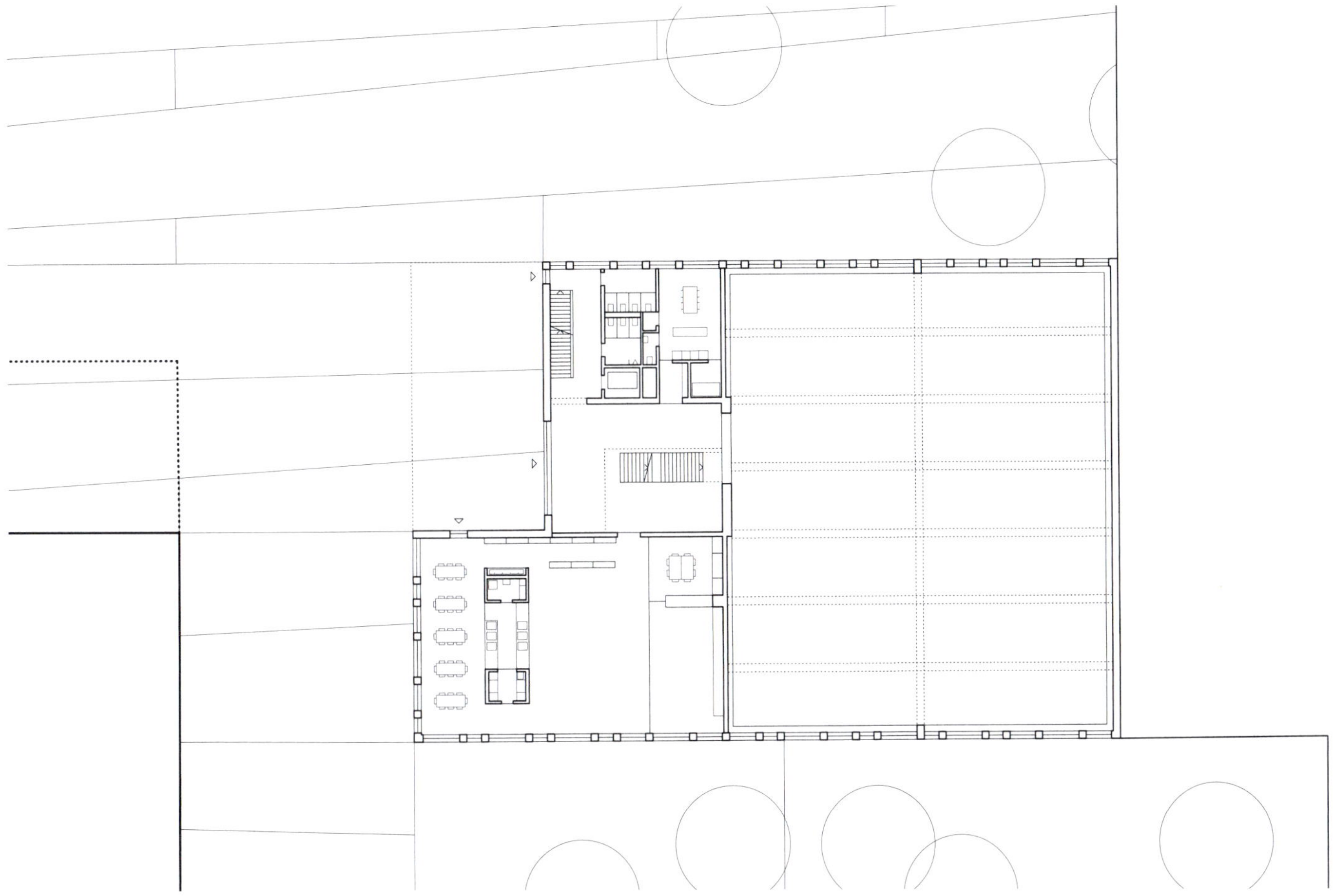

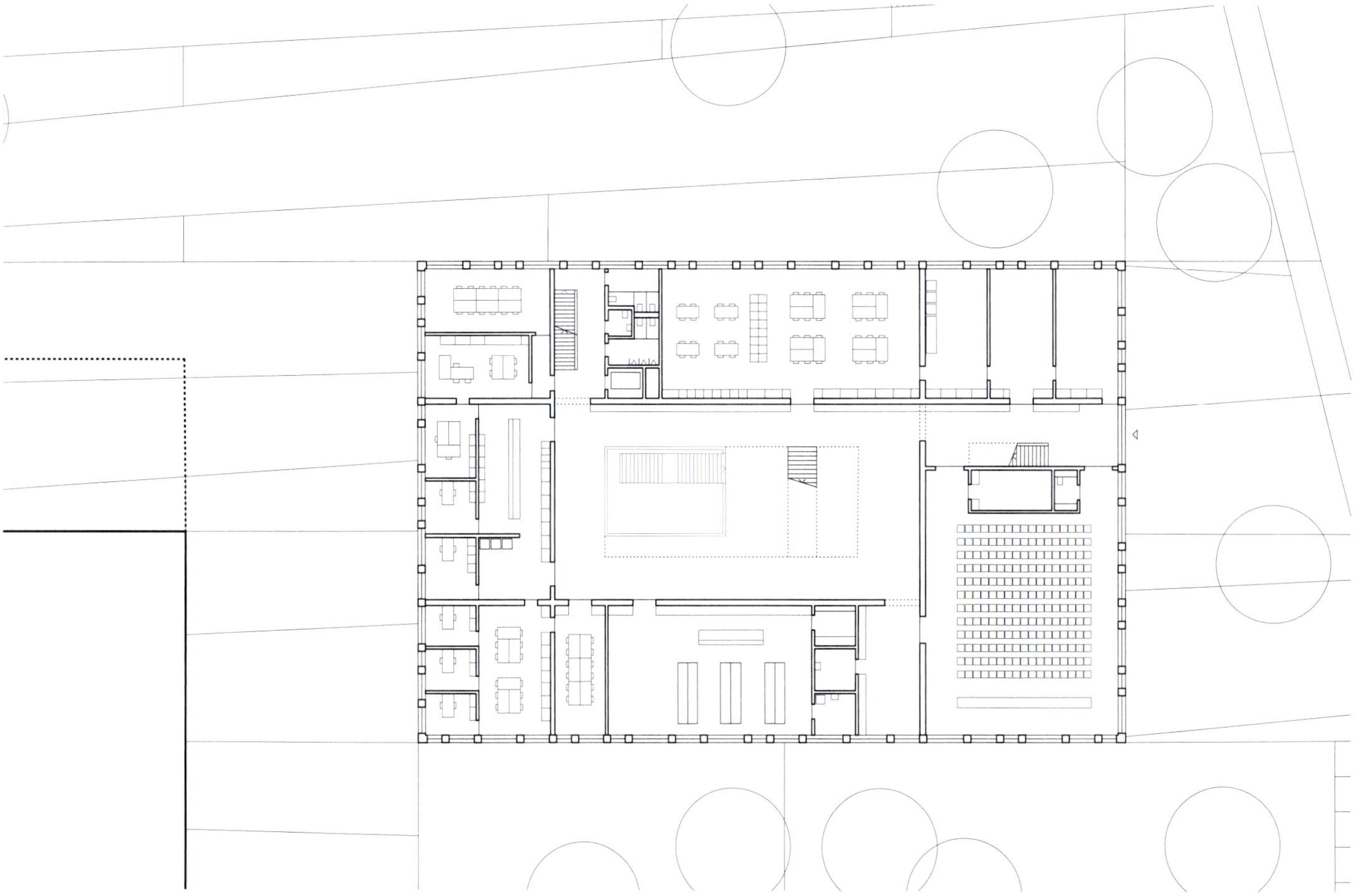

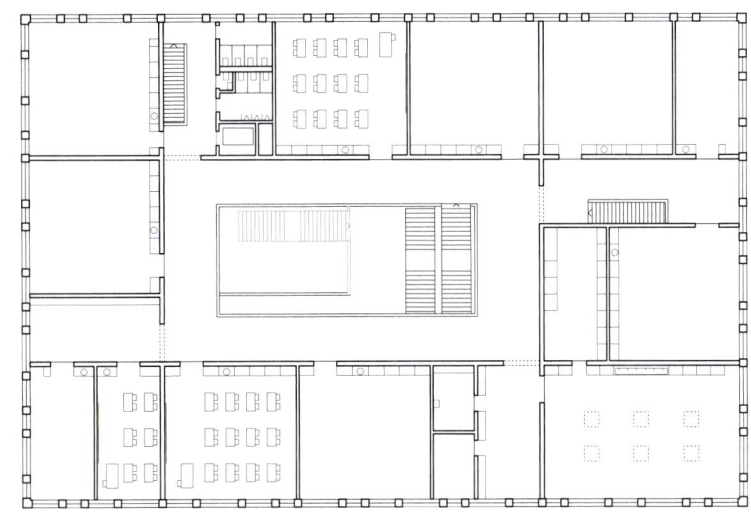

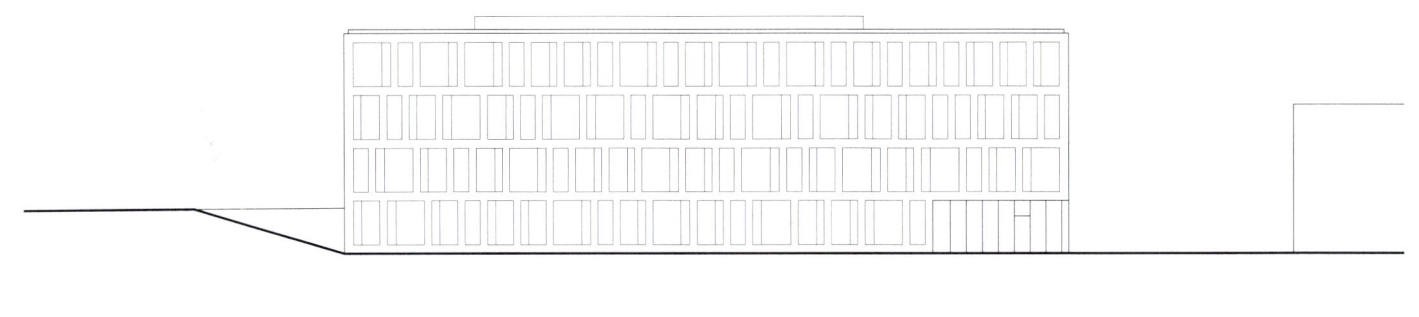

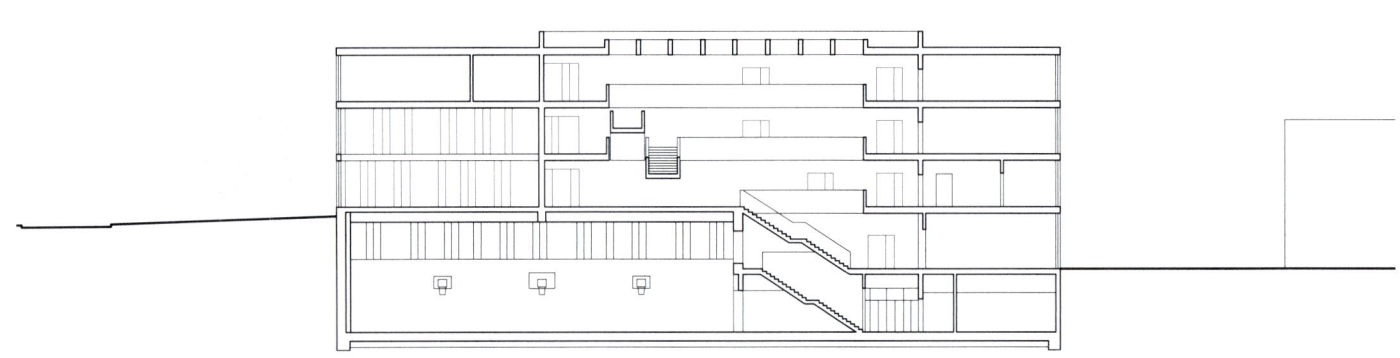

Flugzeugwaschhalle, Payerne

Washing bay, Payerne

Das Volumen der Waschhalle liegt an der südlichen Grenze des Flugplatzes von Payerne und ist so angeordnet, dass der Flächenverbrauch in Bezug auf die bestehende Fahrbahn und die Pisten minimiert wird. Das Gebäude hat eine einfache Konzeption und dient dazu, Flugzeuge und Spezialfahrzeuge mit Druckwasser zu reinigen und das für die Reinigung verwendete Wasser einer biologischen Aufbereitung zuzuführen. Die Einfachheit des Entwurfs – ein einziges rechteckiges Volumen – ist dem Gebrauchszweck angemessen; Gleiches gilt für die Konstruktion (ein Metalltragwerk aus Standardelementen) und die Verkleidung (aus lichtdurchlässigem Polycarbonat, das wasserdicht ist, aber eine natürliche Belichtung des Halleninneren ermöglicht). Die Konstruktion berücksichtigt die Problematik einer nachhaltigen Entwicklung: Alle eingesetzten Materialien können demontiert und wiederverwertet werden, und das Gebäude lässt sich leicht an künftige veränderte Bedürfnisse anpassen. Im Innern der Halle nehmen zwei mit Polycarbonat verkleidete Ädikulä die Betriebseinrichtungen (Büro, Umkleiden, Duschen, WCs) und die Gebäudetechnik (Heizungsanlage, Waschanlage, Wassertanks, Abwasserdepot) auf.

Located at the southern edge of Payerne Airfield, the washing bay was designed to limit the surface to be cleared in relation to the existing roads and runways. The simple building is designed for use in the high-pressure washing of planes and special vehicles while also facilitating the biological treatment of runoff water from the washing process. The simplicity of the design – a single, rectangular building – is suitable for the intended use, as are the structural components (a metal frame consisting of standardised elements) and the type of shell (translucent, waterproof polycarbonate through which the bay is lit by natural sunlight). The construction incorporates sustainable development considerations: all the materials used can be dismantled and recycled while the building can easily be adapted to a range of different needs in the future. Inside, the utility rooms (office, changing rooms, showers, WC) and technical facilities (boiler room, washing installation, tanks, washing product storage area) are housed in 2 kiosks covered in polycarbonate.

Wettbewerb / Competition: 2004
Ausführung / Construction: 2006–2007
Mitarbeit / Collaborators: Mikhail Broger, Gian Serena, Anne Krins
Bauherrschaft / Client: armasuisse
Bauleitung / Construction management: R. Delaporte
Bauingenieur / Structural engineer: R. Beylouné
Bauphysik / Structural physics: Sorane SA
Elektroplanung / Electrical planning: Ing & Tech. SA
Heizungs- und Lüftungsplanung / Heating and ventilation planner: Pierre Chuard Ingénieurs Conseils SA
Sanitärplanung / Sanitary planning: O. Tinelli

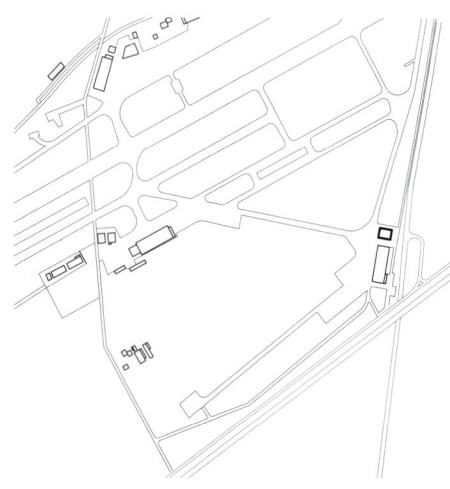

33

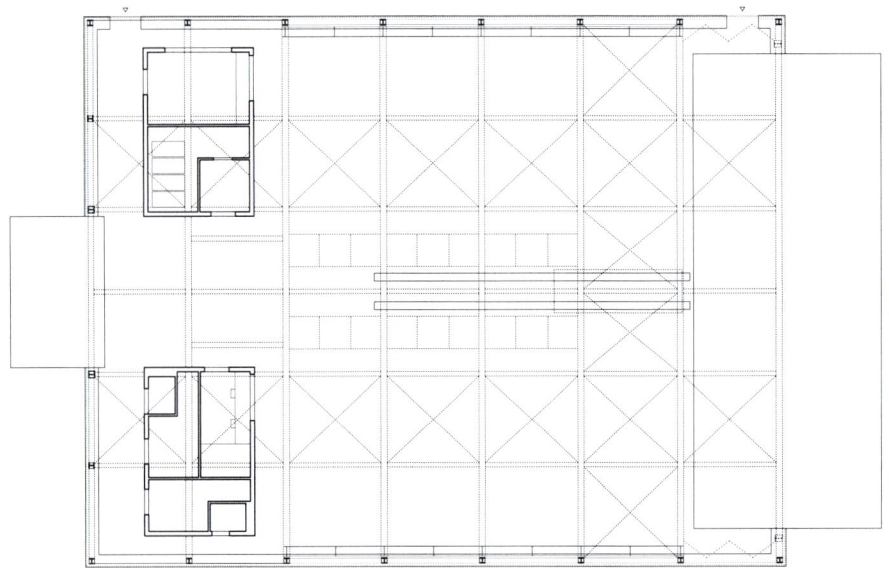

10 m

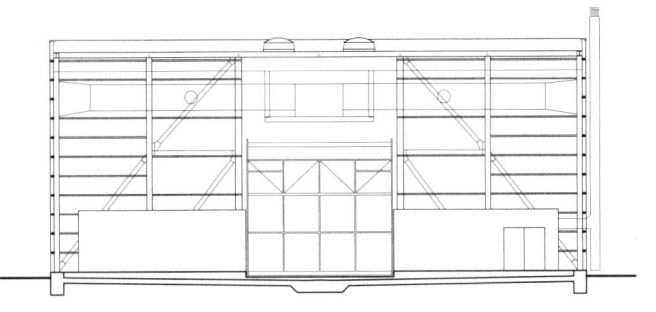
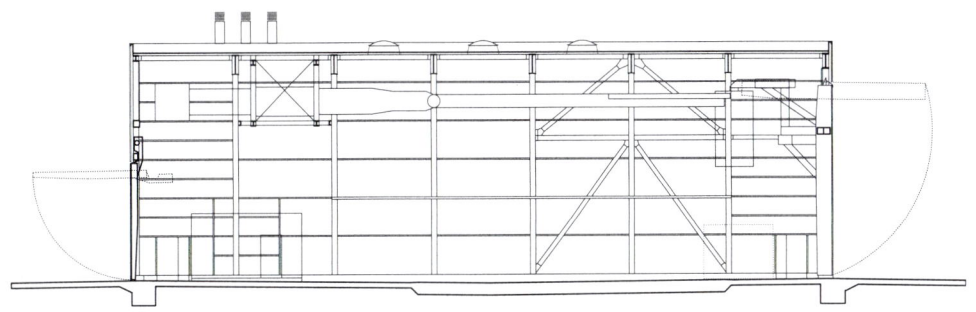

Studentenwohnheime, Saint-Sulpice

Student accommodation, Saint-Sulpice

Das Projekt befindet sich in einem Villenviertel unterhalb der Kantonalstrasse auf einem Gelände, das sich in sanft abfallender Neigung zum Genfersee erstreckt. Das Programm verteilt sich auf vier Volumina in Bajonettform, zwischen denen grosse begrünte Flächen, die sich zum See hin öffnen, «dahinfliessen». Die vorgeschlagene städtebauliche Figur ermöglicht die natürliche Belichtung aller Verkehrs- und Begegnungsflächen; diese öffnen sich nach Süden, während alle Zimmer nach Osten oder Westen ausgerichtet sind. Durch die Verschiebung der Volumina können die diversen Wohneinheiten um ein gemeinsames Treppenhaus gruppiert werden. Die Bajonettgestalt greift die beiden auf dem Gelände vorhandenen Geometrien – einerseits die der Gebäude der EPFL, andererseits die senkrechte Orientierung zum Hang und seinen Höhenlinien – auf und unterstreicht sie. Die Beschränkung der Gebäudehöhe auf vier Etagen sorgt für einen bescheidenen Massstab und erlaubt eine bessere Integration der Bauten in den Kontext. Im Innern wurde den Erschliessungswegen und Fluren besondere Aufmerksamkeit gewidmet, darüber hinaus auch dem Entwurf der Zimmer, die sich durch einen grosszügigen Fensterbalkon nach aussen vergrössern.

The project blends into a cityscape of villas and small housing blocks located below the cantonal road on a plot of land sloping gently down towards Lake Geneva. The programme is divided into four buildings in a bayonet-shaped layout with large, green areas "flowing" between them and overlooking the lake. The location and layout ensure that all the pathways and south-facing gathering points are bathed in natural light, with the rooms located to the east and west. The offset design of the different buildings clearly identifies the different groups of rooms arranged around a shared stairwell. The layout reflects and emphasises the two different geometries present on the site: that of the EPFL buildings and that of the orientation perpendicular to the slope with its curved levels. Choosing to limit the height of the buildings to 4 floors ensured that they blended seamlessly into the surrounding landscape. Inside, particular attention was paid to the hallways and open areas as well as to the design of the rooms, which boast a large window and balcony.

Wettbewerb / Competition: 2006
Ausführung / Construction: 2008–2009
Bauherrschaft / Client: Coopérative d'habitation Les Estudiantines
Mitarbeit / Collaborator: Mikhail Broger
Umsetzung / Implementation partners: FarraFazan
Generalplaner / General planner: Karl Steiner SA
Bauingenieur / Structural engineer: Synaxis SA
Heizungs- und Lüftungsplanung / Heating and ventilation planner: Pierre Chuard Ingénieurs Conseils SA
Sanitärplanung / Sanitary planning: Duschein SA
Landschaftsarchitekt / Landscape architecture: L'Atelier du Paysage Jean-Yves Le Baron sàrl

20 m

Wohn- und Pflegeheim Bois-Gentil, Lausanne

Bois-Gentil residential and nursing home, Lausanne

Das Pflegeheim Bois-Gentil II besteht aus 56 geriatrischen Plätzen, verteilt auf vier Stationen mit 14 Betten, die zwei Versorgungseinheiten bilden. Eine Krippe für 22 Kinder und eine Tiefgarage ergänzen das Programm. Das Gebäude befindet sich auf einem schmalen, lang gestreckten Grundstück mit starker Neigung, das von der Villa Diserens dominiert wird, einem bürgerlichen Familienwohnsitz vom Anfang des 20. Jahrhunderts. Das Projekt konzentriert sich auf den unteren Teil des Geländes und belässt die Villa Diserens als frei stehendes Gebäude.

Das Grundstück wird als ein zusammenhängender Garten behandelt; die beiden Gebäude können als Solitäre innerhalb eines grossen Parks verstanden werden, dessen Eigenart und dessen grosse Bäume erhalten wurden. Das neue Gebäude präsentiert sich als ein Ensemble aus zwei Volumina auf einem gemeinsamen Sockel, dessen Massstab zu den Nachbargebäuden passt. Der in den Hang hineingebaute Sockel nimmt die Gemeinschaftsaktivitäten des Pflegeheims auf. Die erhöht liegende Eingangszone gewährt Zugang zur Rezeption und zur Kinderkrippe und weiter zum Restaurant sowie zu anderen Gemeinschaftsbereichen, die den Kern der Einrichtung darstellen. Als Erweiterung des Restaurants öffnet sich eine Terrasse gen Süden und stellt eine Beziehung zum Garten her. Die Zimmer des Pflegeheims nehmen die vier obersten Etagen des Gebäudes ein; sie sind um ein gemeinsames Treppenhaus herum angeordnet.

The Bois-Gentil II residential and nursing home comprises 56 geriatric nursing beds divided into 4 living units of 14 beds, forming two care units. The project also includes a nursery for 22 children and an underground car park. The complex is located on a long, narrow, steeply sloping plot of land overlooked by the "Diserens" villa, a large, turn-of-the-century house. The project focussed on the lower section of the plot without disturbing the "Diserens" villa. The land was seen as a continuous garden in which the two buildings are perceived as separate elements in a large park which has retained its character and its main trees. The complex is divided into two entities set on a base and is built on a scale which is entirely in keeping with the neighbouring structures. Built into the slope, the base houses the shared activities of the home. The raised entrance provides access to the reception and nursery and, further on, to the restaurant and other communal areas of the project, which form the beating heart of the institution. The south-facing terrace outside the restaurant creates a relationship with the garden. The rooms are located on the top four floors of the building and are built around a shared stairwell.

Wettbewerb / Competition: 2004
Ausführung / Construction: 2009–2010
Bauherrschaft / Client: Fondation Bois-Gentil, Etat de Vaud (Service de la Santé publique)
Mitarbeit / Collaborators: Mikhail Broger, Diane de Pourtalès, Cécile Bertrand, Andrew Hugonnet
Bauleitung / Construction management: R. Bruchez
Bauingenieur / Structural engineer: Frey & Associés
Bauphysik / Structural physics: Sorane SA
Elektroplanung / Electrical planning: Louis Richard SA
Heizungs- und Lüftungsplanung / Heating and ventilation planner: Chammartin & Spicher SA
Sanitärplanung / Sanitary planning: Saniplans SA
Landschaftsarchitekt / Landscape architecture: L'Atelier du Paysage Jean-Yves Le Baron sàrl
Lichtkonzept / Lighting design: Aebischer & Bovigny

43

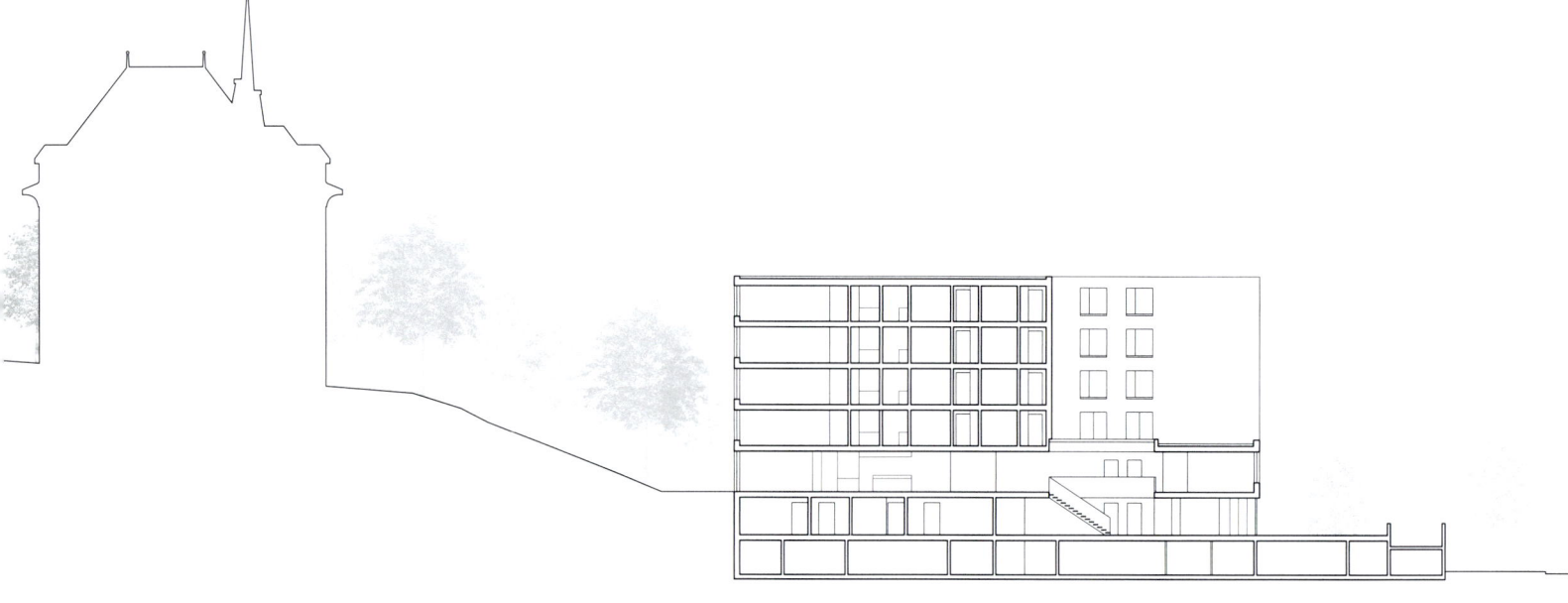

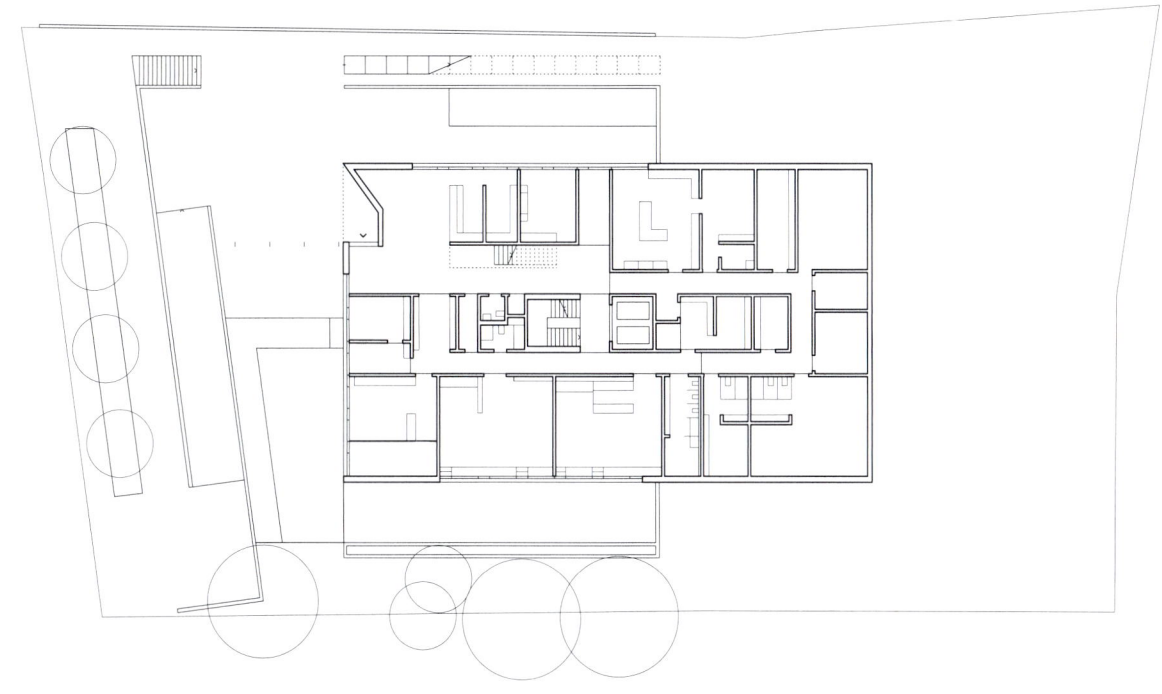

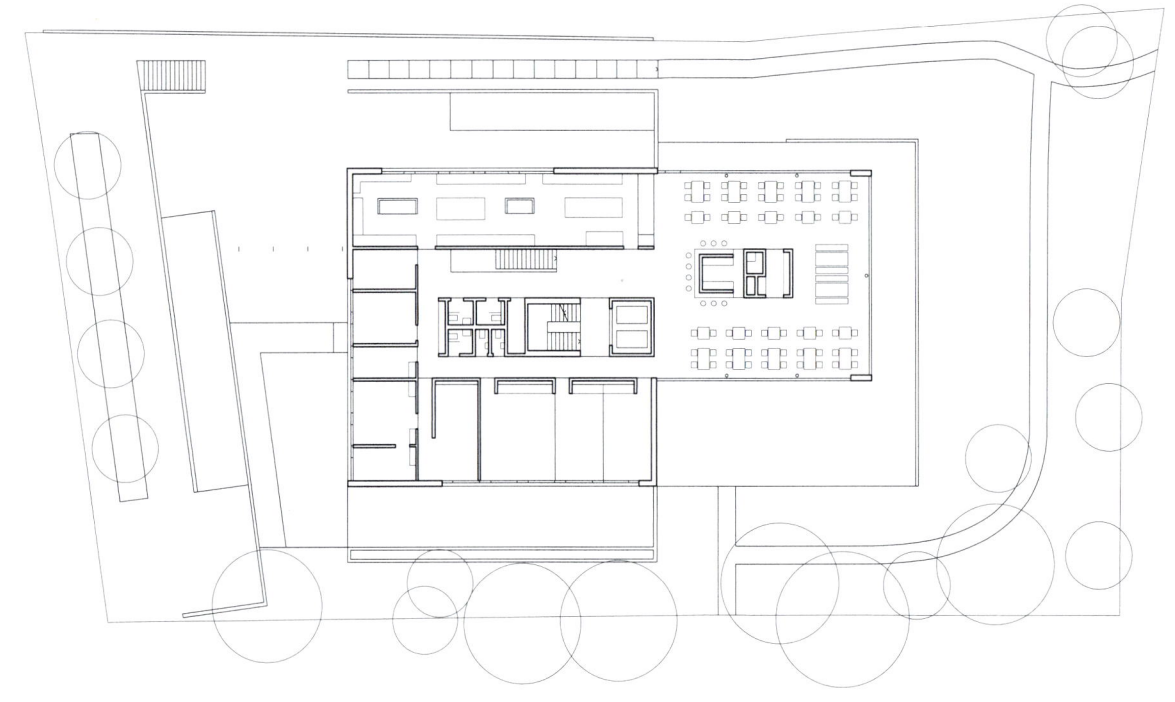

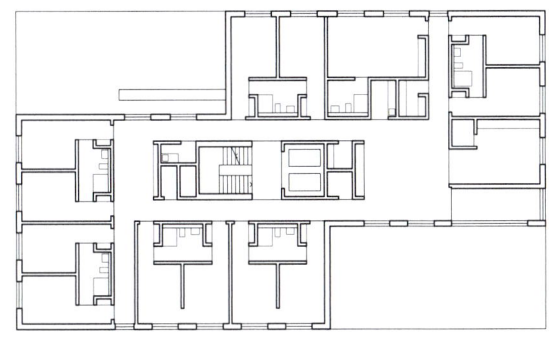

Wohn- und Pflegeheim Le Marronnier, Lutry

Le Marronnier residential and nursing home, Lutry

Das Gelände, das sich zum Genfersee und zu den Französischen Alpen öffnet, wird von einem alten Mädchenpensionat dominiert, das im Jahr 1900 von Georges Épitaux errichtet wurde und den Ausgangspunkt der Komposition bildet. Der frühere Vordereingang wurde verändert, um Platz für eine leicht geneigte Rampe zu schaffen, die bis hinauf zur Ebene des Zugangshofs führt. Der Komplex zeigt sich als Ensemble aus drei Volumina, die durch eine gemeinsame Terrasse verbunden sind. Das Gebäude von Épitaux bleibt erhalten und wird zum Angelpunkt dieser Komposition. Durch diese Verteilung werden unterschiedliche Ausrichtungen sowie Gärten für die verschiedenen Einheiten möglich: der Eingangshof, ein gesicherter Garten für die Psychogeriatrie, ein öffentlicher, sich zum See und zu den Alpen öffnender Garten und private Gärten. Die drei Versorgungseinheiten (Geriatrie, Psychogeriatrie, Abteilung zur vorübergehenden Aufnahme) sind jeweils in einem der drei Volumina untergebracht und im Erdgeschoss durch einen Sockel verbunden, der die gemeinschaftlichen Flächen aufnimmt. Dieser Ort ist als ein «Dorfplatz» konzipiert, eine Stätte der Begegnung und des geselligen Austauschs. Man findet dort eine Bar, einen Friseursalon, eine Kaminecke und das Restaurant, welches sich zu einer beschatteten Terrasse mit Blick auf den See öffnet.

Overlooking Lake Geneva and the French Alps, the site is dominated by a former girls' boarding house built in 1900 by George Epitaux, which served as the starting point for the project. The former front access was modified to form a gently sloping ramp leading to the level of the entrance courtyard. The construction is divided into three buildings connected by a shared, inhabited terrace. Epitaux's building was retained and forms the fulcrum of the project. The design incorporates orientations and gardens for the different entities: an entrance courtyard, a secure garden for the psycho-geriatric department, a public garden overlooking the lake and the Alps, and private gardens.
The three care units (geriatrics, psycho-geriatrics and the temporary accommodation unit) are each housed in one of the three different buildings and connected on the ground floor by an area containing the communal facilities. This area is designed as a "village square", a place where meeting and interaction is encouraged by means of a bar, a hair salon, a fireplace area and a restaurant which opens onto a shady terrace overlooking the lake.

Wettbewerb / Competition: 2003
Ausführung / Construction: 2012–2014
Bauherrschaft / Client: EMS Le Marronnier
Mitarbeit / Collaborators: Omar Trinca, José Garrazza, Albert Pons, Anne Krins
Bauingenieur / Structural engineer: Giacomini & Jolliet SA
Bauphysik / Structural physics: Sorane SA
Elektroplanung / Electrical planning: Louis Richard SA
Heizungs- und Lüftungsplanung / Heating and ventilation planner: Chammartin & Spicher SA
Sanitärplanung / Sanitary planning: Saniplans SA
Landschaftsarchitekt / Landscape architecture: L'Atelier du Paysage Jean-Yves Le Baron sàrl
Lichtkonzept / Lighting design: Aebischer & Bovigny

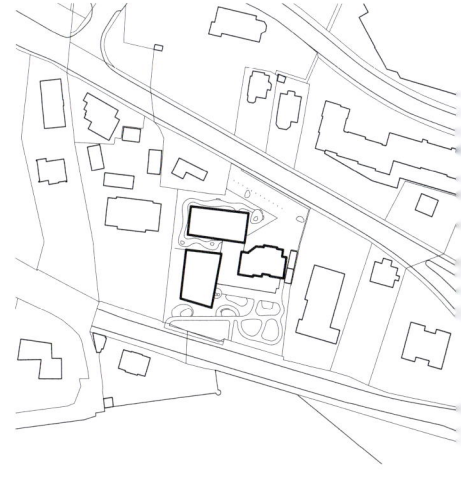

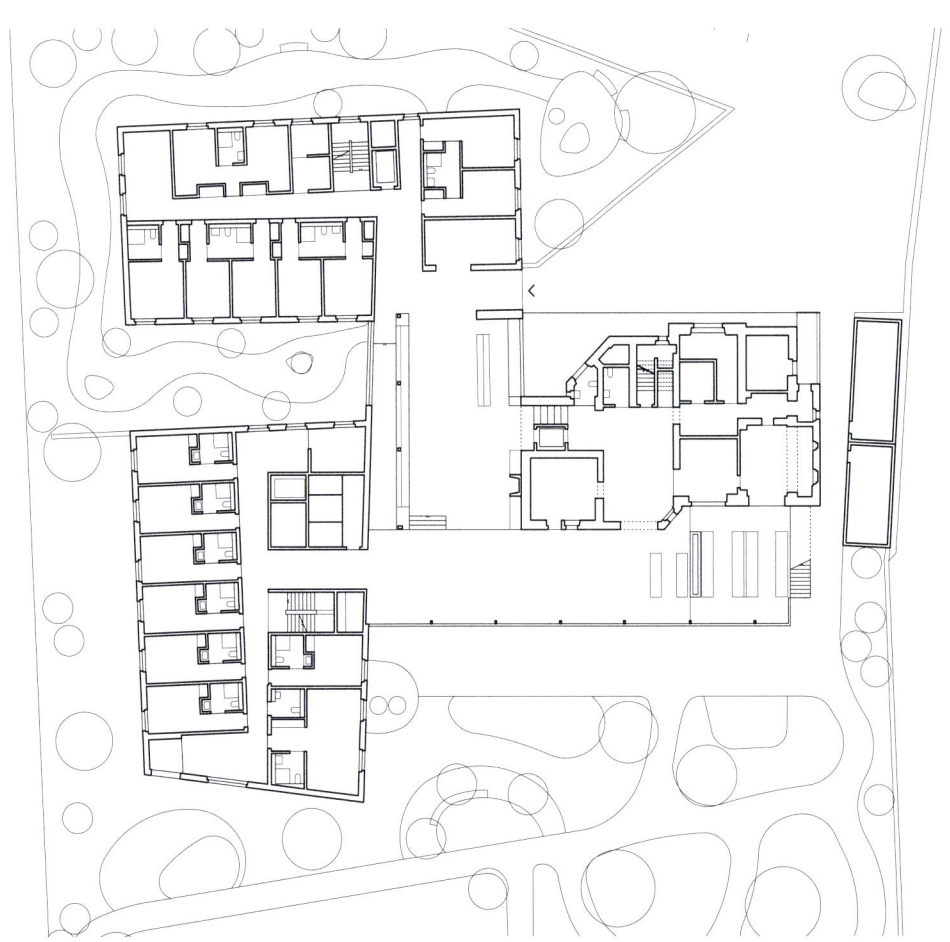

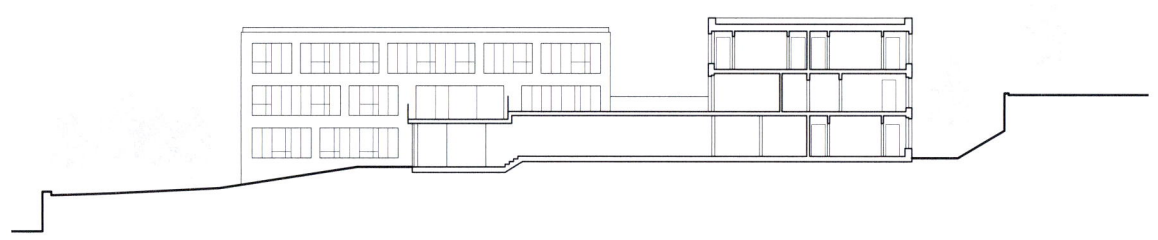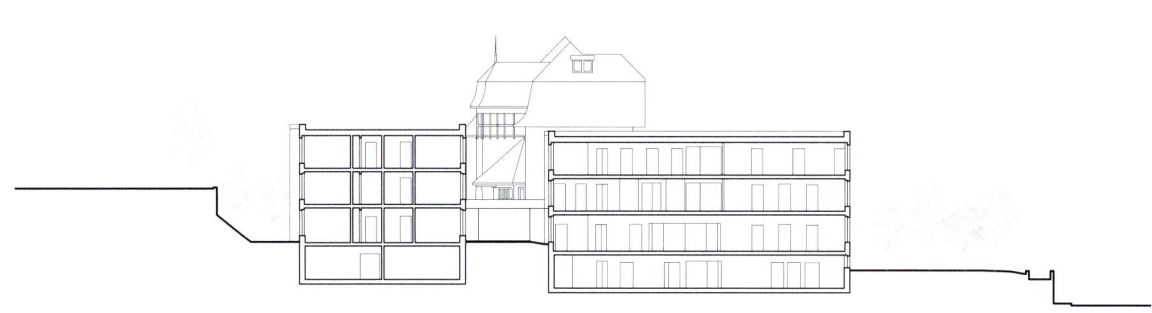

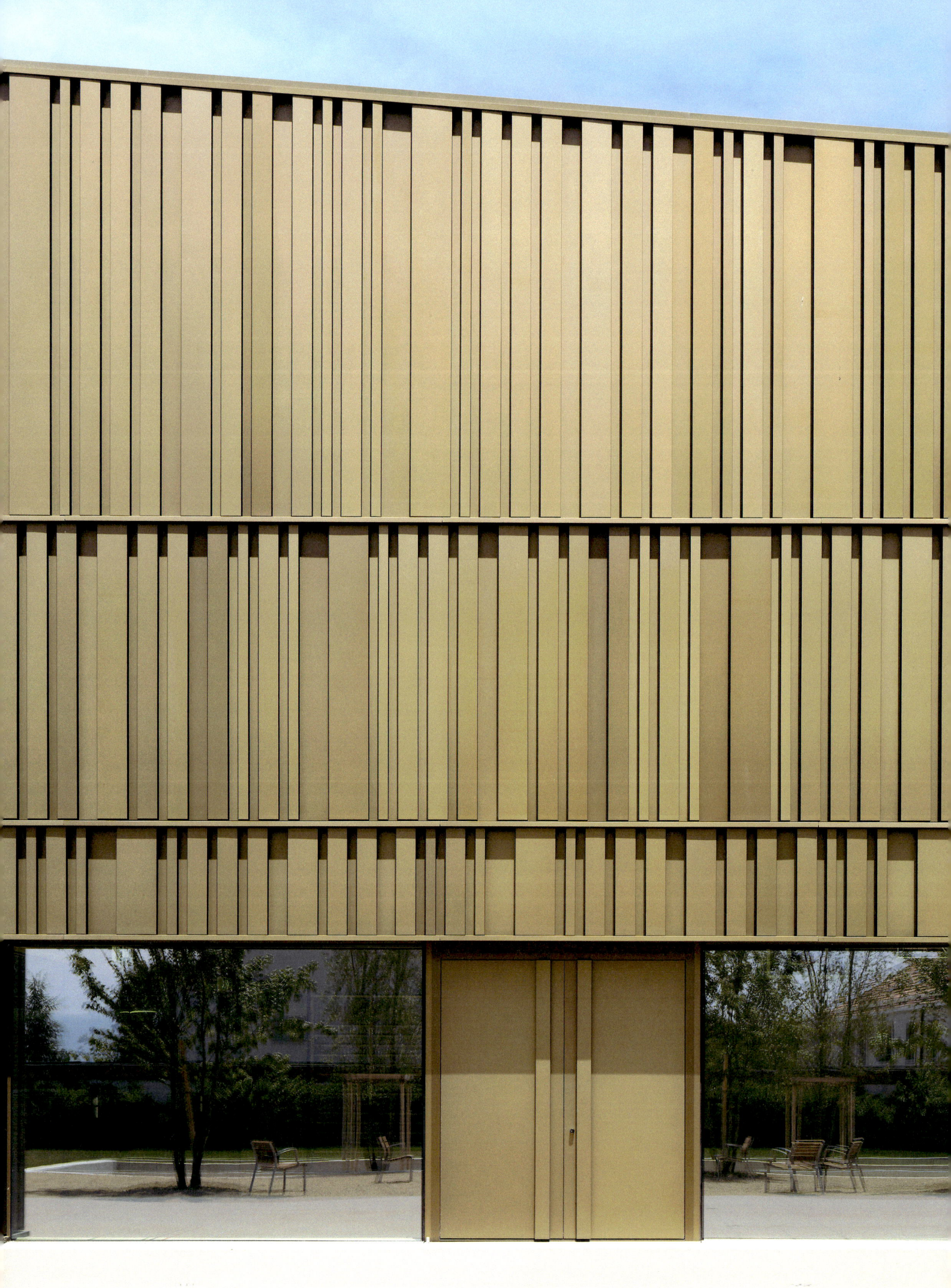

Gemeindehaus, Chavannes-des-Bois

Municipal building, Chavannes-des-Bois

Unter dem Gelände, welches das Gemeindehaus und eine Kinderkrippe aufnimmt, befindet sich ein Zivilschutzbunker. Weitere Bauten könnten in Zukunft die beiden neuen öffentlichen Einrichtungen rund um ein neues Dorfzentrum ergänzen. Die versetzte Positionierung der verschiedenen Gebäude schafft Aussenräume von unterschiedlicher Form und individuellem Charakter, die gegeneinander verschoben sind. Das Gemeindehaus wurde auf einem Teil des bestehenden Zivilschutzbunkers errichtet. Der Grundriss des Gemeindehauses wurde so gestaltet, dass die Deckplatte des Schutzraums nicht belastet wird. Im Erdgeschoss setzt sich das Foyer in einem grossen geschützten Überhang fort, der sich zum Dorfplatz und weiter zum Jura öffnet, während die Mehrzweckhalle sich zu einem nach Süden gerichteten Platz öffnet. Von Norden ist ein Zugang zu den in der östlichen Etage untergebrachten Büros der Gemeindeverwaltung möglich.

Die Erschliessungsflure münden im grosszügig angelegten und sich zur Fassade hin öffnenden Treppenhaus. Sie enden im doppelgeschossigen Foyer und setzen somit die verschiedenen Eingänge miteinander in Beziehung.

Housing a municipal building and a nursery, the site also includes an underground civil defence shelter. Other buildings could be added to these two public facilities built around a new village square. The offset layout of the different buildings creates outside areas boasting different shapes and characters which are nevertheless in harmony with one another. The municipal building is built on part of the existing civil defence shelter. The plan of the municipal building was designed to avoid overloading the shelter block. On the ground floor, the centre is complemented by a broad covered area opening onto the village square and overlooking the Jura, while the multi-purpose hall opens onto a south-facing square. The municipal administration offices on the upper floor can be accessed from the north.

The corridors serving the different elements of the project boast large open areas on the façade or open onto the main area of the complex with its double ceiling height, thereby joining the different access points to the site.

Wettbewerb/Competition: 2010
Ausführung/Construction: 2011–2014
Bauherrschaft/Client: Gemeinde Chavannes-des-Bois/ Municipality of Chavannes-des-Bois
Mitarbeit / Collaborators: Deirdre McKenna, Ruben Sousa, Xaveer Gheysens, Jeanne Garcia
Bauleitung/Construction management: a.planir sàrl
Bauingenieur/Structural engineer: Boss & associés
Elektroplanung/Electrical planning: Mab Ingénierie SA
Heizungs-, Lüftungs- und Sanitärplanung / Heating, ventilation and sanitary planner: AZ ingénieurs
Landschaftsarchitekt/Landscape architecture: L'Atelier du Paysage Jean-Yves Le Baron sàrl
Lichtkonzept/Lighting design: Aebischer & Bovigny

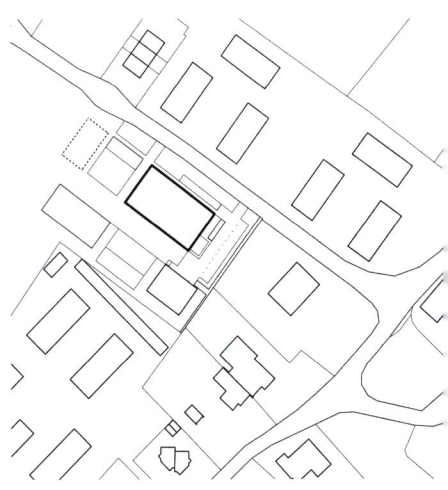

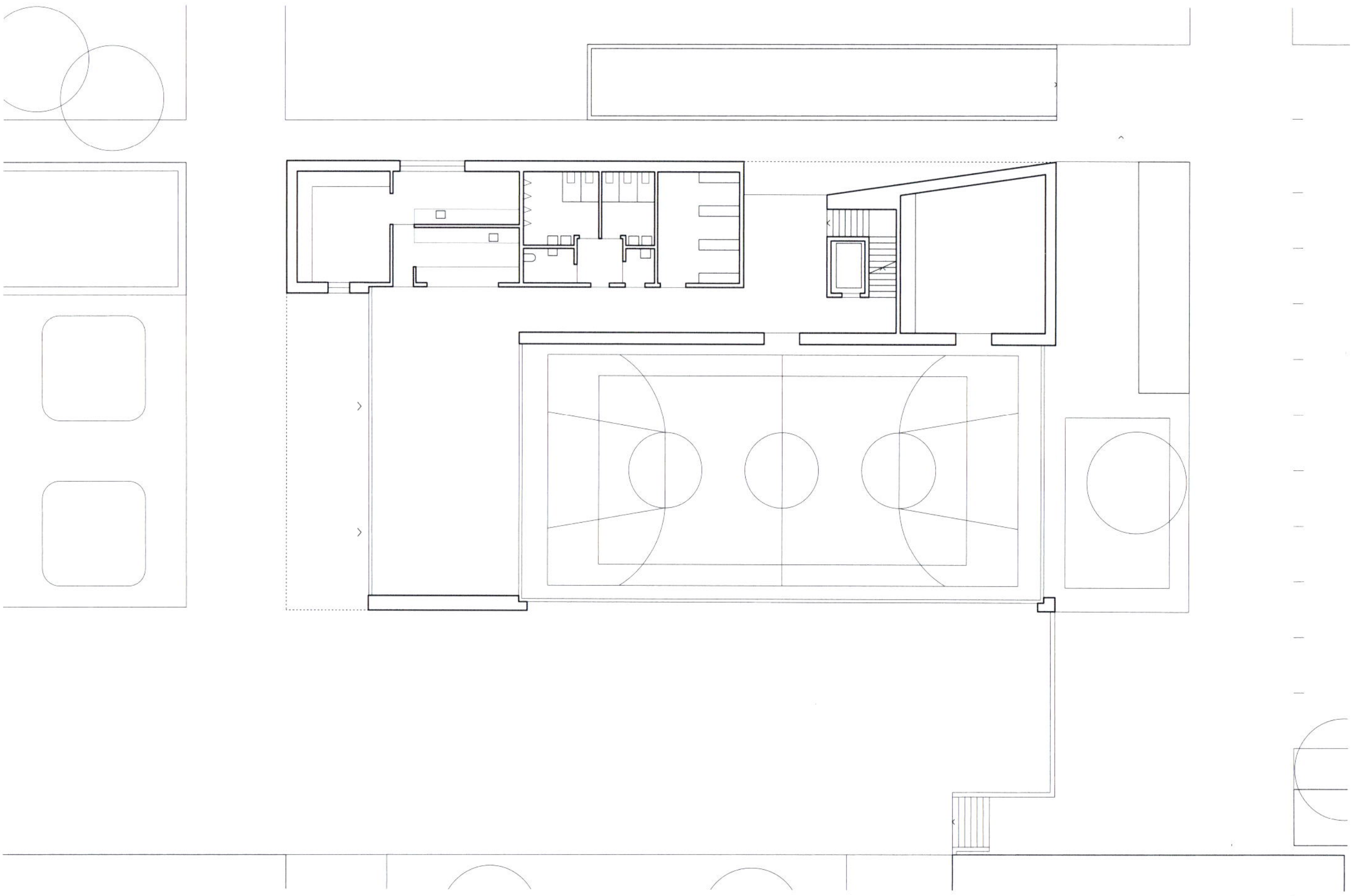

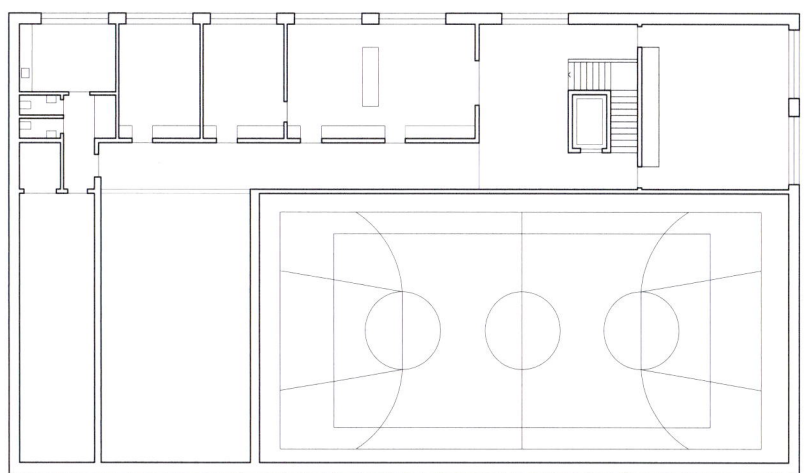

10 m

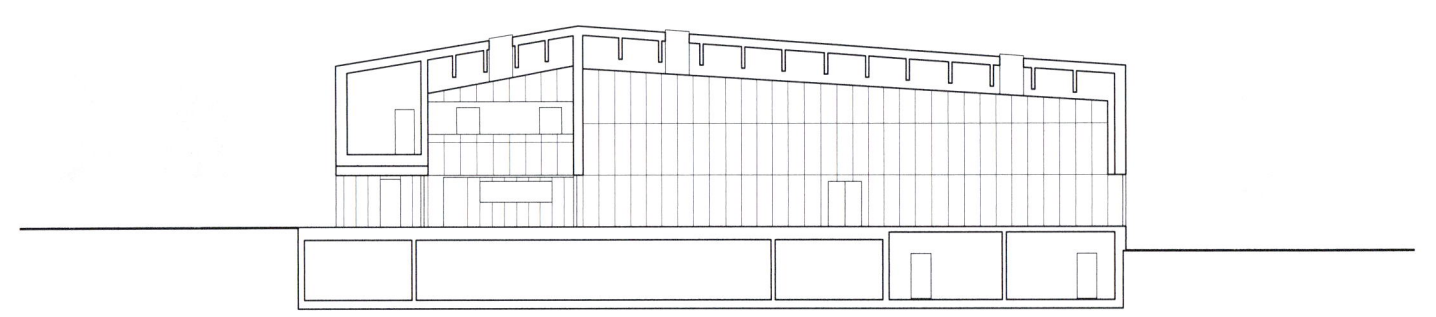

Wohn- und Pflegeheim Pré-Fleuri, Lausanne

Pré-Fleuri residential and nursing home, Lausanne

Das Gebäude des Pflegeheims Pré-Fleuri befindet sich im Südwesten der Parzelle, im Innern eines Gebiets mit vier weiteren Wohngebäuden. Das Pflegeheim umfasst 53 Betten in 47 Einzel- und drei Doppelzimmern sowie begleitende Räumlichkeiten, die zur Erfüllung des psychogeriatrischen Zwecks der Einrichtung erforderlich sind. Die unterschiedlichen Räume verteilen sich auf ein Untergeschoss und fünf Etagen darüber, von denen das oberste das Attikageschoss einnimmt. Im Erdgeschoss sind die Gemeinschaftsflächen und die Verwaltung des Pflegeheims untergebracht. Das Restaurant öffnet sich mit einer Terrasse nach draussen. Das Untergeschoss nimmt alle Technikräume und eine Tiefgarage auf. In den Obergeschossen sind die Zimmer zur Fassade orientiert; die Betriebsräume und die Erschliessungswege befinden sich in der Mitte. Letztere öffnen sich mittels kleiner Aufenthaltsräume oder Freiflächen zur Fassade. Diese Freiflächen gewähren Ausblicke nach draussen und sorgen zugleich für eine natürliche Belichtung der Erschliessungswege. Die Gemeinschaftszonen sind so verteilt, dass den Bewohnern verschiedene Räume hinsichtlich Dimension und Orientierung angeboten werden. Jeder dieser Räume erhält eine spezifische Einrichtung. Im Attikageschoss befinden sich fünf Zimmer und Gemeinschaftsflächen für die gesamte Einrichtung.

The Pré-Fleuri residential and nursing home building is located at the south-west corner of the plot of land within a development area comprising 4 other housing units. The residential and nursing home accommodates 53 beds in 47 single rooms and 3 double rooms, as well as the support facilities necessary for the psycho-geriatric role of the institution. The different areas are spread across 1 basement level and 5 above-ground levels including the top attic level. The ground floor houses the communal areas and administrative offices of the home. The restaurant has an outdoor terrace. The technical facilities and car park are located in the basement. On the upper floors, the rooms are located along the façade with the utility rooms and corridors at the centre of the building. The latter nevertheless open onto the façade by means of small lounges or open areas offering a view of the surrounding area and increasing the light filtering into the hallways. The communal areas are designed to offer residents several areas of different sizes and orientation, each boasting their own features. The attic floor comprises 5 rooms and communal areas intended for the institution as a whole.

Projekt/Projet: 2009
Ausführung/Construction: 2012–2014
Bauherrschaft/Client: Résidence Pré-Fleuri EMS
Mitarbeit/Collaborators: Marjolaine Obrist, Cécile Bertrand, Jeanne Garcia, Marta Ruis Penas, Claire Rosat
Bauleitung/Construction management: Regtec SA
Bauingenieur/Structural engineer: Giacomini & Jolliet SA
Elektroplanung/Electrical planning: Louis Richard SA
Heizungs- und Lüftungsplanung/Heating and ventilation planner: AZ Ing. Conseils SA
Sanitärplanung/Sanitary planning: H. Schumacher Ing. Conseils SA
Landschaftsarchitekt/Landscape architecture: L'Atelier du Paysage Jean-Yves Le Baron sàrl
Lichtkonzept/Lighting design: Aebischer & Bovigny

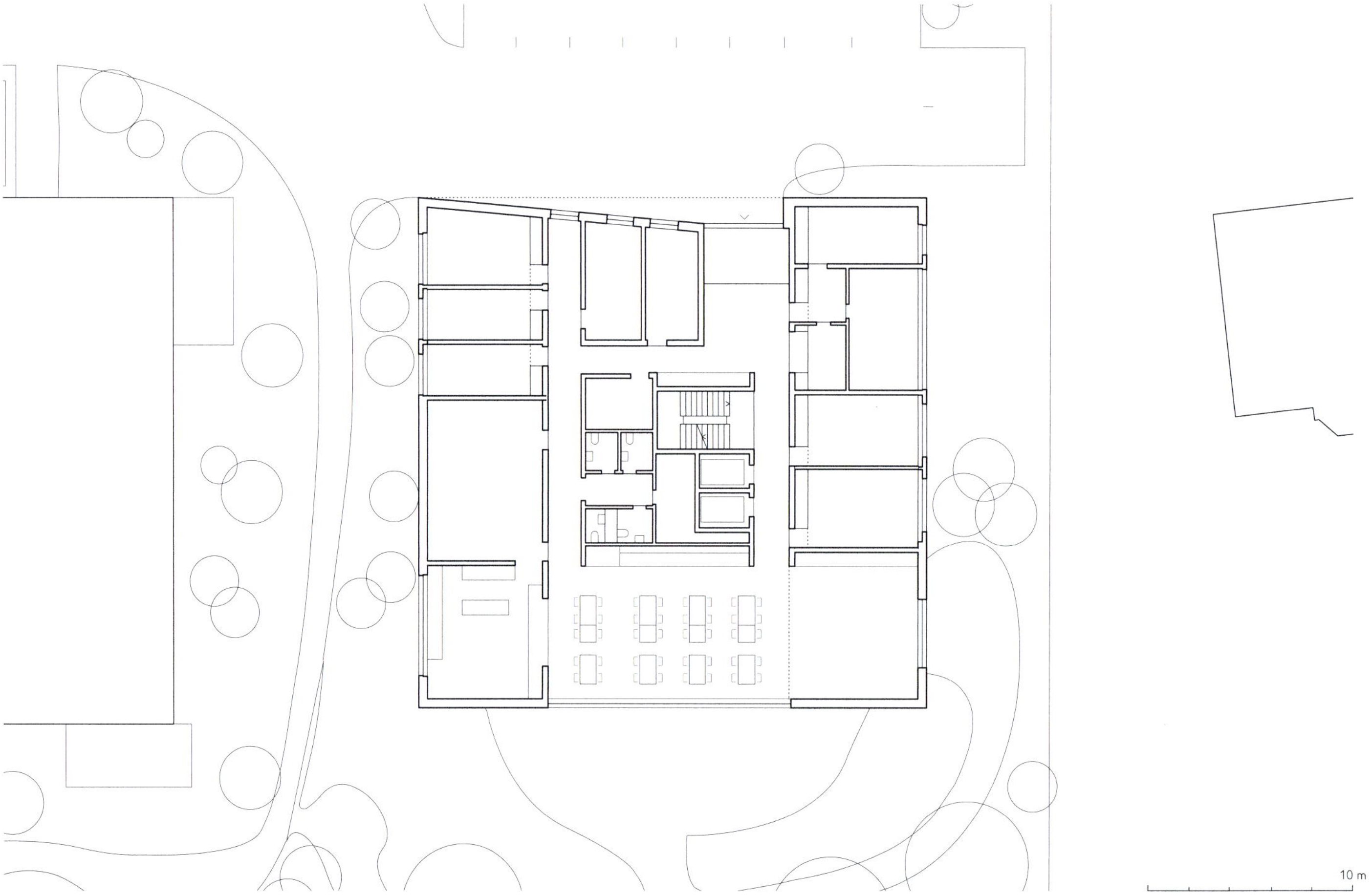

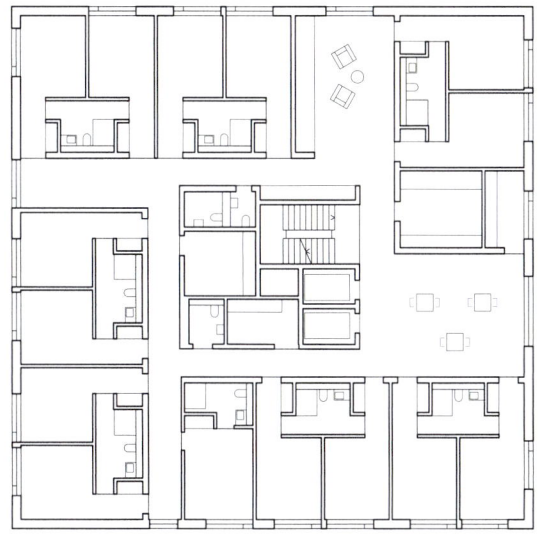

Censuy-Schule, Renens / Censuy School, Renens

Das Grundstück der Censuy-Schule liegt zwischen der Rue du Lac im Norden und dem Parkplatz von Censuy im Süden in einem Gebiet, das von öffentlichen Einrichtungen und Sportanlagen bestimmt ist. Eine Reihe von Wohnungen begrenzt die Parzelle nach Nordwesten. An ihnen entlang verläuft ein alter schmaler Weg, der den Parkplatz mit dem Schulgelände und im Weiteren mit den Wohnvierteln verbindet.

Das Projekt möchte die Bedeutung dieses «Schulwegs» deutlich machen. Daher wurde entlang des Wegs der Schulhof angelegt, um den sich die anderen schulischen Gebäude verteilen: das bestehende Schulgebäude, die neue Schule und die Sporthallen, die in direkter Beziehung zu dem bestehenden Sportplatz stehen. Dieses neue einheitliche Ensemble ermöglicht es, auf dem Rest der Parzelle einen Fussballplatz und Sportanlagen für die Einwohner des Viertels anzulegen.

Die Klassenzimmer sind auf gegenüberliegenden Seiten eines Versorgungskerns verteilt, der an beiden Schmalseiten grosse, zur Fassade offene Freiräume lässt, die sich für verschiedene Aktivitäten eignen. Die in den Boden abgesenkten Sporthallen sind unterirdisch mit dem Schulgebäude verbunden.

The site of Censuy School is located between Rue du Lac to the north and the Censuy car park to the south, in a neighbourhood characterised by public buildings and sports facilities. A series of accommodation units border the plot to the west, along which a narrow path links the car parks to the school site and the inhabited areas further on. The project aims to highlight the importance of this "schoolchildren's path" by building the school yard alongside it with the other school buildings arranged around the yard: the existing school, the new school and the sports halls directly adjacent to the existing sports area. This new homogenous complex leaves room for a football pitch and a sports park for the local inhabitants.

The classrooms are arranged around a service block, creating a large area at each end opening onto the façade which can be used for a range of different activities. The semi-underground sports halls are connected to the school building by the basement.

Wettbewerb / Competition: 2011
Ausführung / Construction: 2012–2015
Bauherrschaft / Client: Stadt Renens / Ville de Renens
Mitarbeit / Collaborators: Deirdre McKenna, Ruben Sousa, Xaveer Gheysens, Jeanne Garcia
Bauleitung / Construction management: Regtec SA
Bauingenieur / Structural engineer: Amsler & Bombelli & associés
Elektroplanung / Electrical planning: Perrin & Spaeth
Heizungs- und Lüftungsplanung / Heating and ventilation planner: AZ ingénieurs SA
Sanitärplanung / Sanitary planning: Tecsan
Landschaftsarchitekt / Landscape architecture: L'Atelier du Paysage Jean-Yves Le Baron sàrl
Lichtkonzept / Lighting design: Aebischer & Bovigny

20 m

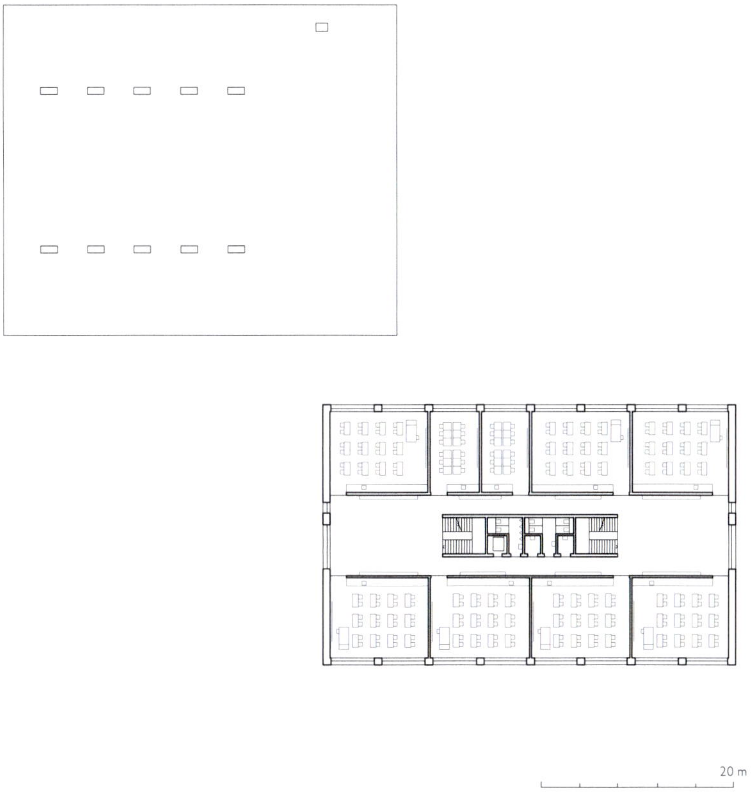

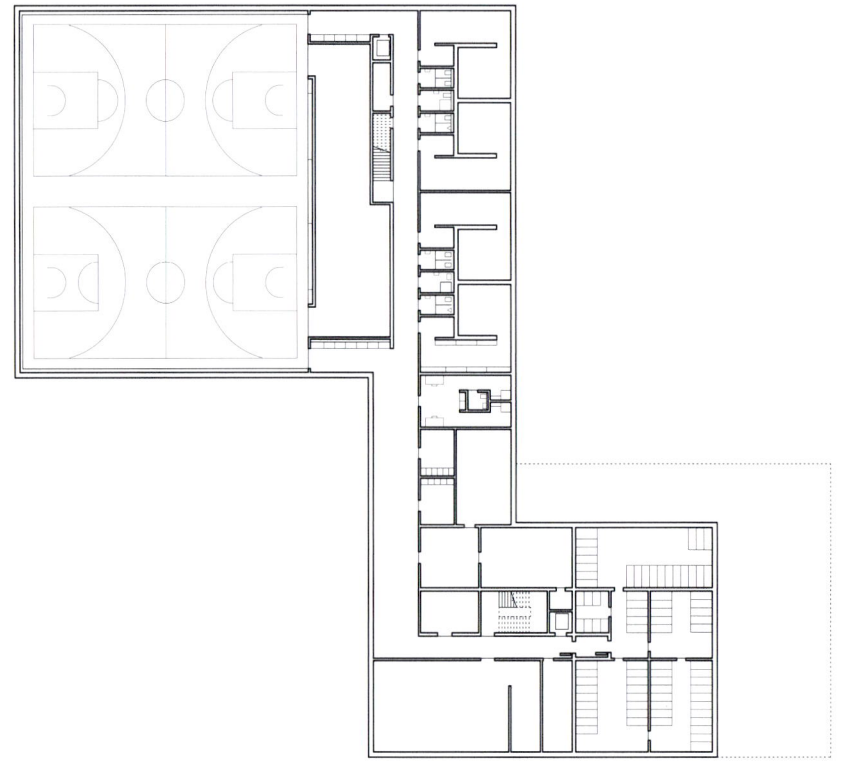

Stadtvilla Chailly, Lausanne

Chailly urban villa, Lausanne

In einem uneinheitlichen städtischen Umfeld präsentiert sich das neue Gebäude aus Sichtbeton als ein plötzlich aus der Vegetation auftauchender steinerner Monolith, aus dem Terrassen, Loggien und überdachte Bereiche ausgeschnitten sind. Die stark abschüssige Parzelle öffnet sich nach Süden mit schönem Ausblick auf den See und die Berge. Ein über die Fassade belichtetes Treppenhaus erschliesst drei Wohnungen von ähnlicher Grösse. Zwei Wohnungen liegen auf einer Etage; hinzu kommt ein doppelgeschossiges Penthouse. Die Wohnungen haben einen offenen Grundriss, um die Erschliessungsflächen zugunsten der Wohnfläche möglichst klein zu halten. Die Küche und das Wohnzimmer verteilen sich um eine grosse Loggia oder eine nach Süden offene Terrasse mit freiem Ausblick. Jede Wohnung besitzt Fenster nach drei oder vier Seiten. Die Aussenmauern aus Beton sind tragend. Die grossen Fenster öffnen sich zur Landschaft und zum baulichen Kontext. Sie bestehen aus zwei Teilen: einem einfachen Teil für die Belüftung und einem verglasten für die Aussicht und die Belichtung. Der landschaftlich gestaltete Garten besteht aus Terrassen, die in den Hang eingebettet sind. Sie sind teils gepflastert, teils begrünt, sodass vielfältige Nutzungen möglich sind.

Incorporated into a heterogeneous urban fabric, the new building made of rough fair-faced concrete resembles a mineral monolith springing from the vegetation with terraces, loggias and covered areas. Located on a steep slope, the plot is south-facing and offers attractive views over the lake and mountains. A well-lit stairwell on the façade serves three apartments with similar surface areas: two apartments on one level and another duplex apartment in the attic. The apartments have a flowing design, reducing the hallways for the benefit of the living areas. The kitchen and living room are arranged around a large loggia or an open, south-facing terrace with an attractive view. Each apartment enjoys three or four different orientations. The outside concrete walls are load-bearing. The windows are designed as large openings onto the surrounding countryside and cityscape. The windows are divided into two parts: a solid pane for ventilation and a glazed section offering a view and allowing light to enter. The landscaped garden comprises tiered terraces built into the slope – sometimes mineral, sometimes planted – creating specific atmospheres complementing the intended usage.

Projet/Projekt: 2010–2013
Ausführung/Construction: 2013–2015
Bauherrschaft/Client: Privat/private
Mitarbeit/Collaborators: Miguel Pereiro, Claudia Awad
Bauingenieur/Structural engineer: Giacomini & Jolliet SA
Elektroplanung/Electrical planning: Louis Richard SA
Heizungs- und Lüftungsplanung/Heating and ventilation planner: Pierre Chuard Ingénieurs Conseils SA
Sanitärplanung/Sanitary planning: Mayor & Cie SA
Landschaftsarchitekt/Landscape architecture: L'Atelier du Paysage Jean-Yves Le Baron sàrl
Lichtkonzept/Lighting design: Aebischer & Bovigny

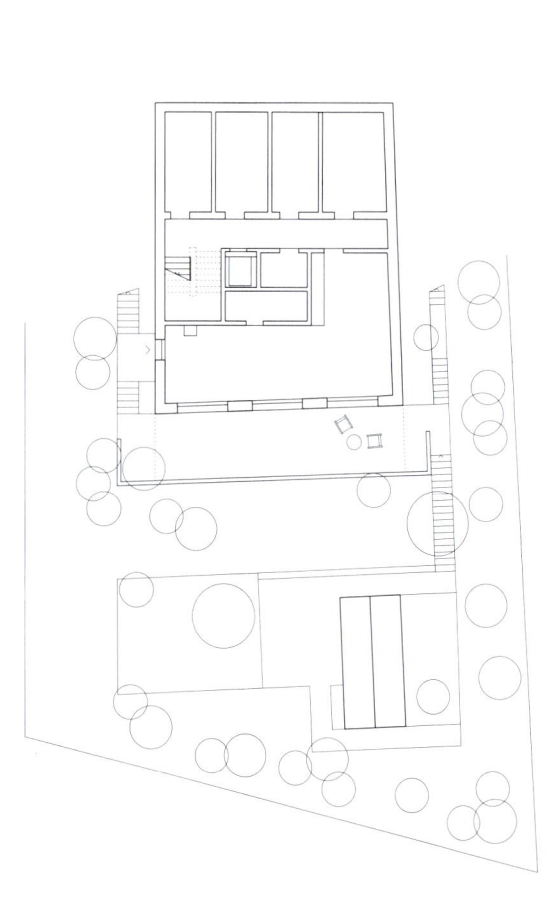
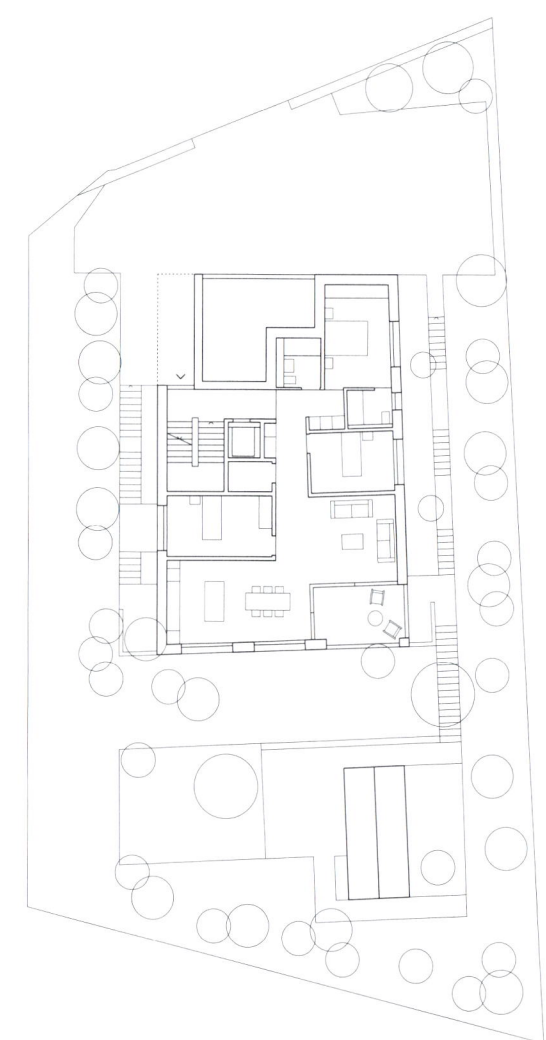

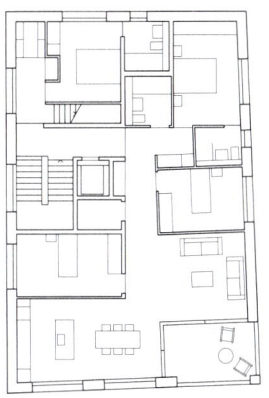
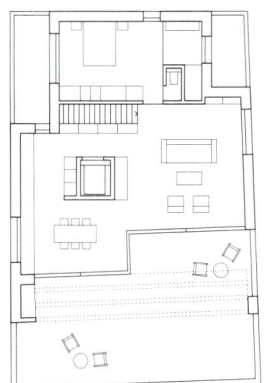

10 m

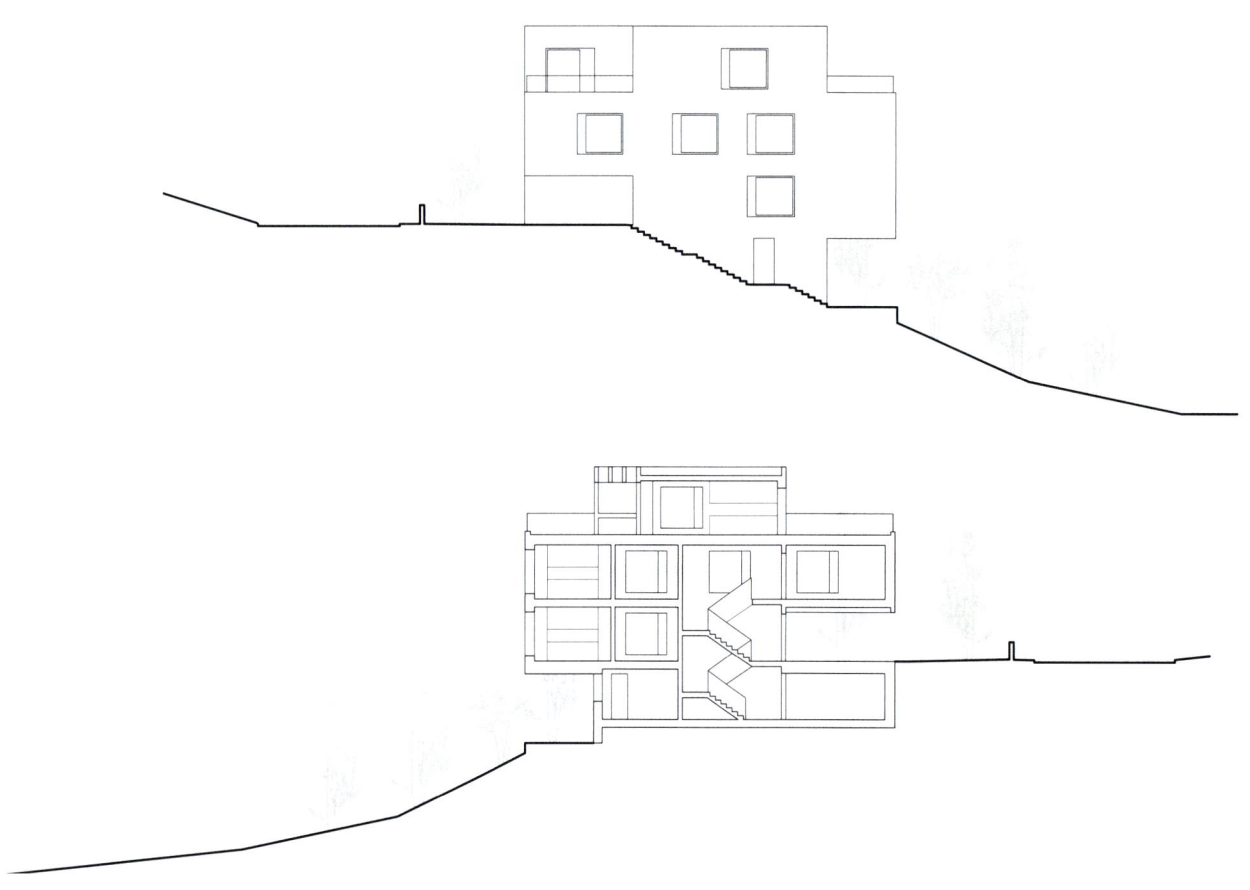

Schulzentrum Mabillon, Monthey

Mabillon school centre, Monthey

Die schulischen und schulergänzenden Gebäude nehmen die beiden Enden des Grundstücks ein. Dadurch bleibt in der Mitte eine grosse Parkfläche mit Bäumen erhalten, unter denen die imposante Silhouette einer 100 Jahre alten Platane hervorsticht. Der Schulweg, der den Park durchquert, setzt die Avenue du Crochetan im Norden mit der Rue Monthéolo im Süden in Beziehung und bindet die in der Mitte des Viertels liegenden Wohnungen an. Das Gebäude, das die Klassenzimmer aufnimmt, und jenes mit den Sporthallen erstrecken sich entlang der Rue du Monthéolo am Eingang zum Gelände. Ein grosser Vorplatz liegt zwischen den beiden unterirdisch verbundenen Gebäuden. Ein offener Patio ermöglicht eine natürliche Belichtung der Musikzimmer im Untergeschoss und dient ausserhalb der Schulstunden als ein autonomer Eingang. Das Restaurant und die Tagesstätte sind in einem Volumen untergebracht, welches den Nordeingang zum Gelände neu definiert. Zusammen mit dem Bauernhof in Vanay grenzt das Gebäude einen grosszügigen Eingangsplatz ab, der in Bezug zur Avenue du Crochetan steht. Die verschiedenen Gebäude passen sich der vorgegebenen Geometrie der Parzelle an, um den Garten zur Geltung zu bringen. Hier bleibt der Bestand an hohen Bäumen erhalten – unter anderem zählt die 100-jährige Platane dazu.

The school and extra-curricular buildings are built at each end of the site in order to maintain a large expanse of wooded parkland at the centre, dominated by the impressive outline of a large, hundred-year-old plane tree. The schoolchildren's path crossing the park connects Avenue du Crochetan to the north and Rue Monthéolo to the south while serving the houses at the heart of the district. The buildings housing the classrooms and sports halls are located along Rue Monthéolo at the entrance to the site. A vast esplanade connects these two buildings which are linked via the basement. An open patio channels natural light for the music rooms in the basement while offering independent access outside school hours. The restaurant and extra-curricular facilities are located in a building that redefines the northern entrance to the site. Together with the farm in Vanay, this building demarcates a large gathering place adjacent to Avenue du Crochetan. The different buildings comply with the restrictive geometry of the plot or highlight the impressive planted areas such as the hundred-year-old plane tree that has been retained.

Wettbewerb / Competition: 2011
Ausführung / Construction: ausstehend / upcoming
Bauherrschaft / Client: Stadt Monthey / Municipality of Monthey
Mitarbeit / Collaborators: Constanze Beer, Cécile Bertrand, Thierry Manasseh
Bauleitung / Construction management: GayMenzel
Bauingenieur / Structural engineer: ESM Ingénieurs Associés
Bauphysik / Structural physics: Physeos SA
Elektroplanung / Electrical planning: Emeltec sàrl
Heizungs- und Lüftungsplanung / Heating and ventilation planner: Michellod-Clausen SA
Sanitärplanung / Sanitary planning: Saniplans techniques sanitaires SA
Landschaftsarchitekt / Landscape architecture: L'Atelier du Paysage Jean-Yves Le Baron sàrl

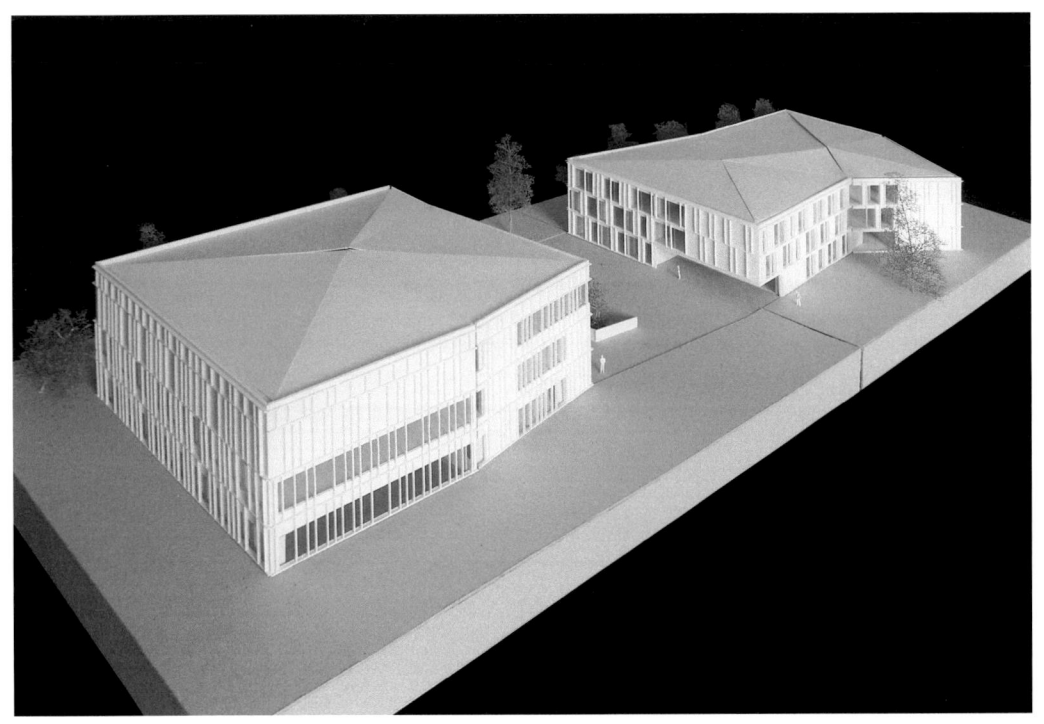

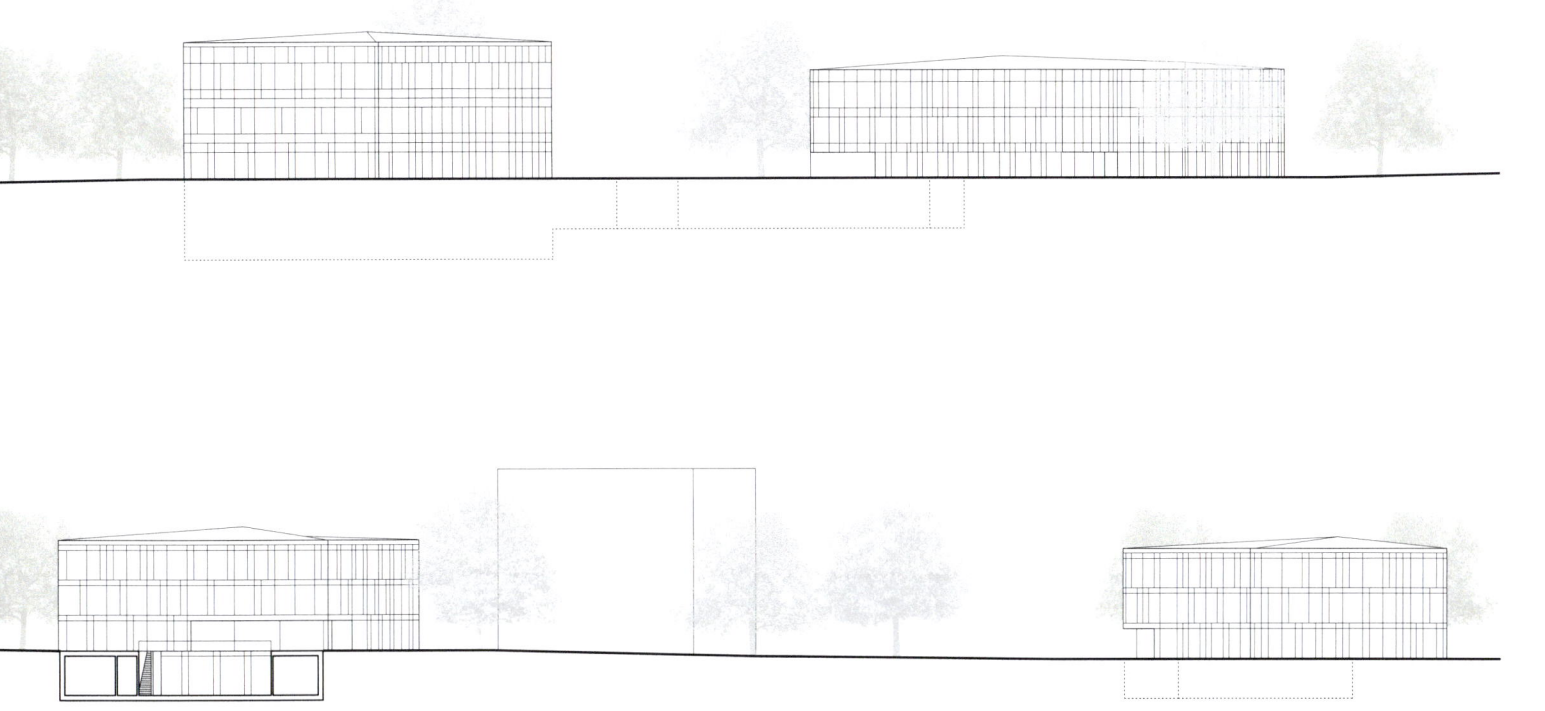

20 m

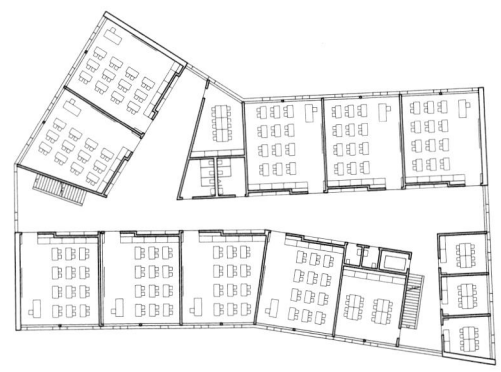 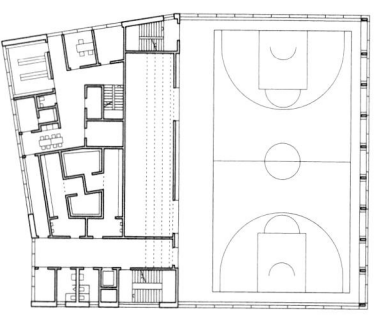

Veranstaltungssaal der *Usine à Gaz* und Wohngebäude, Nyon

Event hall for the *Usine à Gaz* and housing development, Nyon

Der Bebauungsplanplan des Viertels Vy-Creuse-Usine à Gaz-Rive setzte die Rahmenbedingungen für die Volumetrie der Gebäude, eines Theaters mit seinen Serviceflächen im Westen und Wohnungen und Gewerbeflächen im Osten, nahe dem See. Der leicht abfallende, neue öffentliche Platz führt zum Eingang des neuen Theaters. Das Foyer des neuen Theatersaals, die Logen, die Depots, die Verwaltung und der Probensaal verteilen sich in dem Raum zwischen den Gebäuden des alten Theaters und dem neuen Saal, sodass die vorhandenen Örtlichkeiten mit dem künftigen Komplex verbunden sind. Der Theatersaal ist rechteckig, schlicht und funktional. Die Eingänge für Lieferanten und Mitarbeiter des Theaters befinden sich an der Westseite des Gebäudes an der Rue de la Vy-Creuse. Die Künstlerunterkünfte und Büroflächen liegen über dem Theater und sind über eine Erschliessungsstrasse erreichbar. Im östlichen Teil ist das Erdgeschoss Gewerbeflächen vorbehalten. In den beiden Wohnetagen sind 13 Apartments untergebracht, darunter drei durchgehende, grosse im Attikageschoss. Sie verteilen sich um drei offene Innenhöfe, über die Luft und natürliches Licht in das Zentrum des Gebäudes gelangen.

The "Vy-Creuse-Usine à Gaz-Rive" district plan determines the building possibilities precisely, with a theatre and its auxiliary spaces to the west and shops to the east, close to the lake. Built on a gentle slope, the new public square leads to the entrance of the new theatre. The lobby of the new theatre together with the dressing rooms, storage rooms, administrative offices and rehearsal room are housed in the space between the existing theatre buildings and the new theatre, connecting the existing facilities with the future complex. The theatre hall is simple, orthogonal and functional. A tradesmen and artists' entrance is located to the west of the building, connecting with Rue de la Vy-Creuse. The artists' housing and office areas are located above the theatre and can be accessed by a service road. In the eastern section, the ground floor is used for shops. Two floors of accommodation house 13 apartments, with 3 large floor-through apartments in the attic arranged around 3 small open courtyards channelling air and natural light into the very heart of the building.

Wettbewerb / Competition: 2012
Ausführung / Construction: 2016–2018
Bauherrschaft / Client: Stadt Nyon und Privat / Ville de Nyon and private
Mitarbeit / Collaborators: Constanze Beer, Cécile Bertrand, Claire Rosat, Albert Pons
Bauingenieur / Structural engineer: Chabloz & partenaires SA et AB ingénieurs SA
Bauphysik / Structural physics: Sorane SA
Elektroplanung / Electrical planning: Perrin & Spaeth SA, et Tecnoconsult
Heizungs- und Lüftungsplanung / Heating and ventilation planner: Pierre Chuard Ingénieurs Conseils SA et Hirt associés SA
Sanitärplanung / Sanitary planning: H. Schumacher SA et M. Humbert sàrl
Theatertechnik / Stage technology: Changement à vue
Landschaftsarchitekt / Landscape architecture: L'Atelier du Paysage Jean-Yves Le Baron sàrl
Lichtkonzept / Lighting design: Aebischer & Bovigny

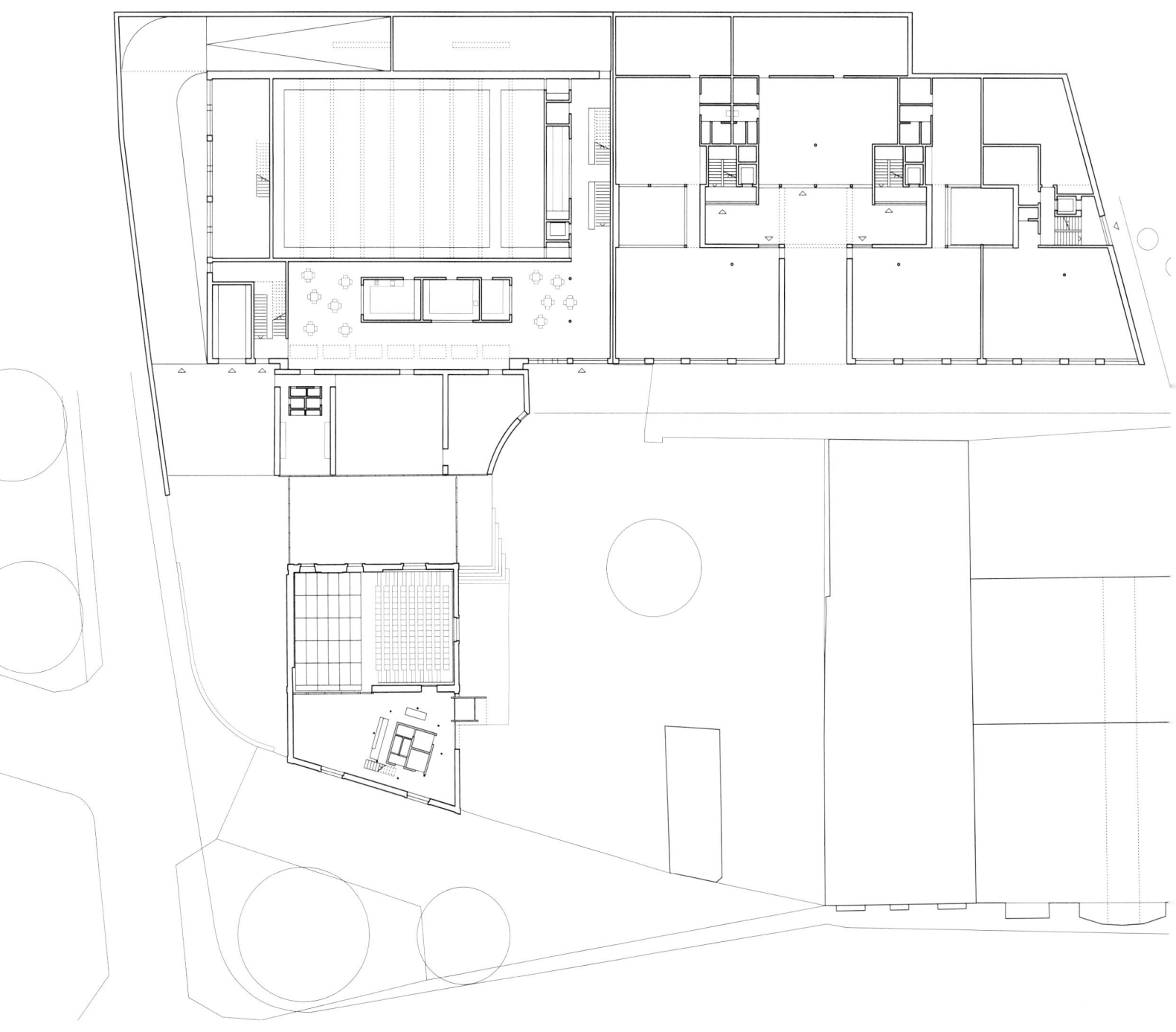

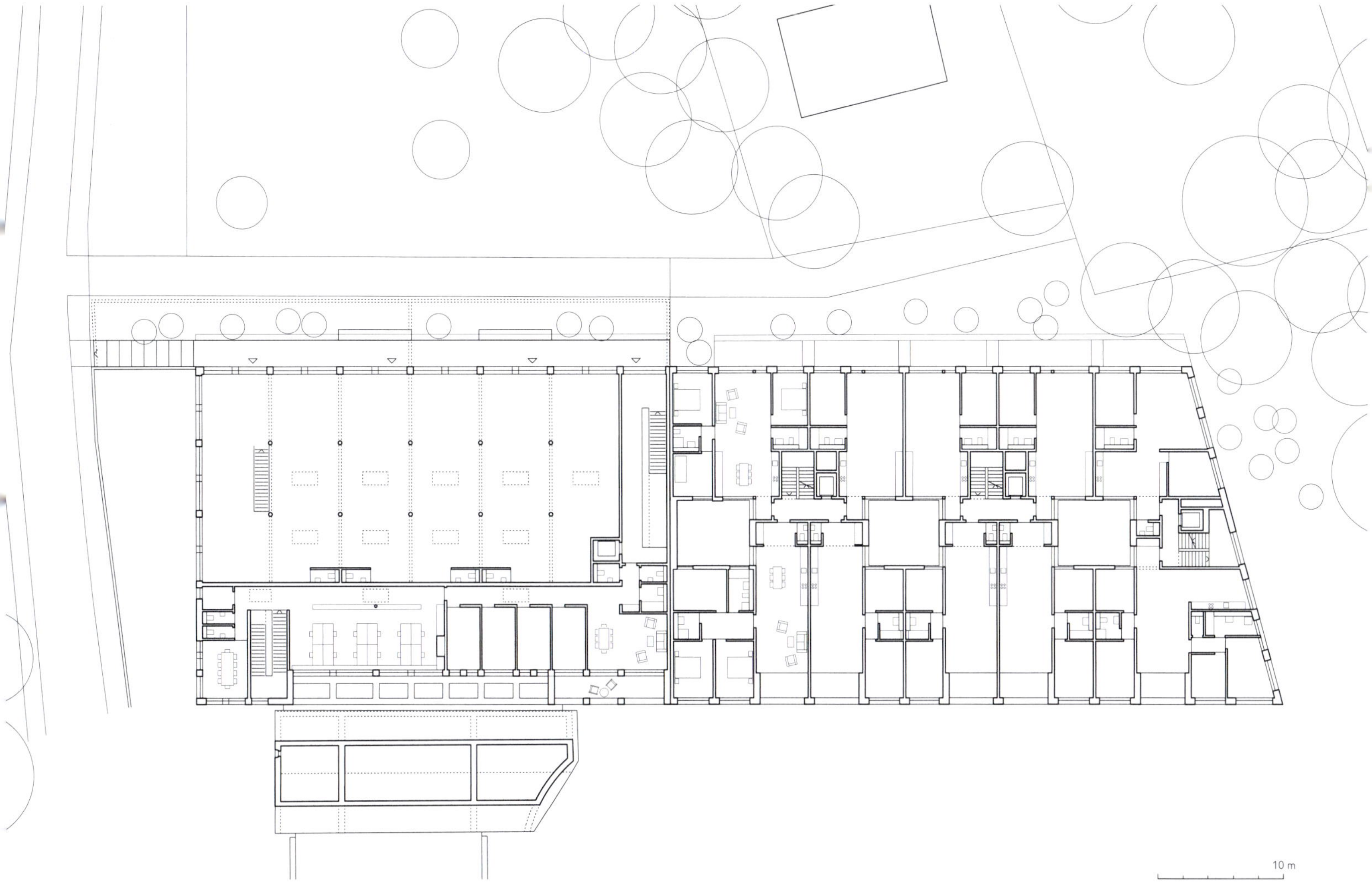

10 m

85

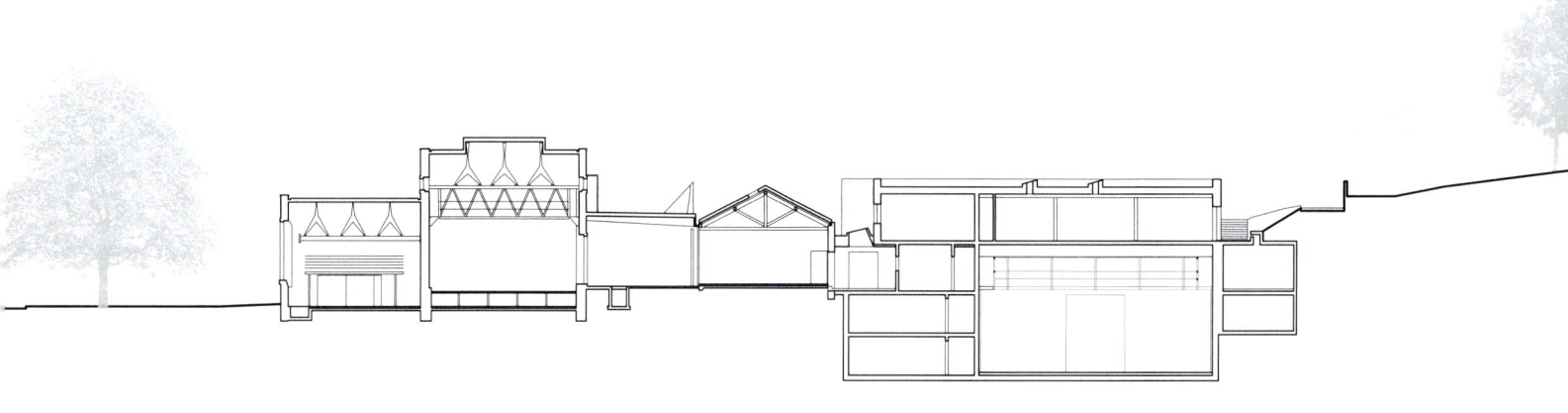

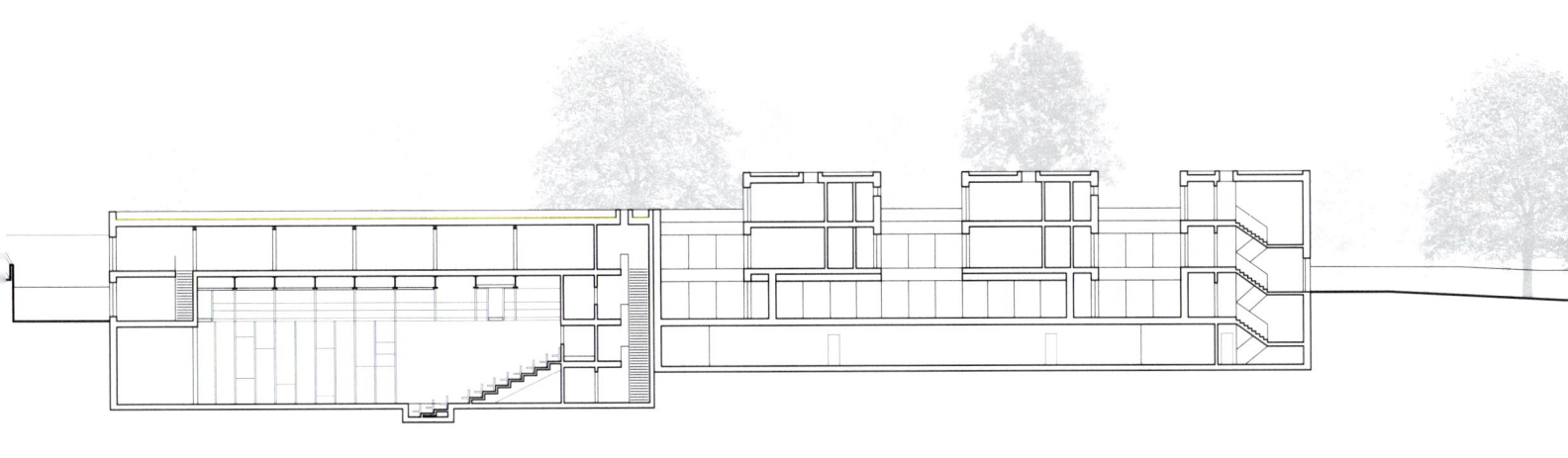

Wohn- und Pflegeheim Les Fauvettes, Montagny-la-Ville
Les Fauvettes residential and nursing home, Montagny-la-Ville

Das Wohn- und Pflegeheim Les Fauvettes liegt auf einem Hügel zwischen dem Tal der Broye und dem Jura im Westen sowie dem Tal der Saane im Osten. Die bestehenden Gebäude sind winkelförmig um einen alten französischen Garten angeordnet, der sich nach Süden zur Landschaft öffnet. Ein grosser Zugangshof verbindet die zum Dorf Montagny-la-Ville führende Strasse mit dem Haupteingang. Die gebrochenen Linien des neuen Gebäudes schliessen an die Verbindungszone zwischen den Bestandsgebäuden – einem alten Waisenhaus und einer Kapelle – an. Die beiden Bauten nehmen alle gemeinschaftlichen Funktionen auf. Die 60 vorgesehenen Zimmer verteilen sich auf drei Wohneinheiten rund um einen grossen zentralen Gemeinschaftsbereich.

Dank der abknickenden Fassaden geniessen alle Zimmer einen Ausblick, ohne von den nahe gelegenen Gebäuden gestört zu werden. Die Erinnerung an den französischen Garten und sein altes Belvedere wird wiederbelebt und zum neuen Landschaftsgarten in Bezug gesetzt, dessen Wege und Plätze sich auf natürliche Weise über das geneigte Gelände schlängeln und die Bewohner zu erholsamen Spaziergängen einladen.

The Les Fauvettes residential and nursing home is located on a hill overlooking the la Broye plain in Fribourg and the Jura to the west, and the foothills of the Alps and the Sarine plain to the east. The existing buildings form an angle around the former French garden opening onto the extensive countryside to the south. A large courtyard provides access to the main entrance from the road leading to the village of Montagny-la-Ville. The broken lines of the new building connect to the area, bringing the existing buildings together, namely a former orphanage and a chapel. The existing buildings house all the communal functions. The 60 rooms included in the project are arranged in 3 living units built around a large, central communal area.

The broken façades ensure all rooms enjoy an attractive view while avoiding irritating views into the nearby existing buildings. The memory of the French garden and its former belvedere are recreated and linked to the new landscaped garden, with the curving paths and squares naturally following the slope of the land, offering residents an ideal place to take a walk or simply relax.

Wettbewerb / Competition: 2013
Ausführung / Construction: 2015–2018
Bauherrschaft / Client: Association des communes pour l'organisation médico-sociale du district de la Broye fribourgeoise
Mitarbeit / Collaborators: Constanze Beer, Ruben Sousa, Deidre McKenna, Albert Pons, Irina Blajev, Aladar Kish
Bauingenieur / Structural engineer: Alberti ingénieurs SA
Bauphysik / Structural physics: Sorane SA
Elektroplanung / Electrical planning: BETELEC SA ingénieurs conseils en électricité
Heizungs- und Lüftungsplanung / Heating and ventilation planner: Dessibourg Energie
Sanitärplanung / Sanitary planning: BESM SA bureau d'études
Landschaftsarchitekt / Landscape architecture: L'Atelier du Paysage Jean-Yves Le Baron sàrl
Lichtkonzept / Lighting design: Aebischer & Bovigny

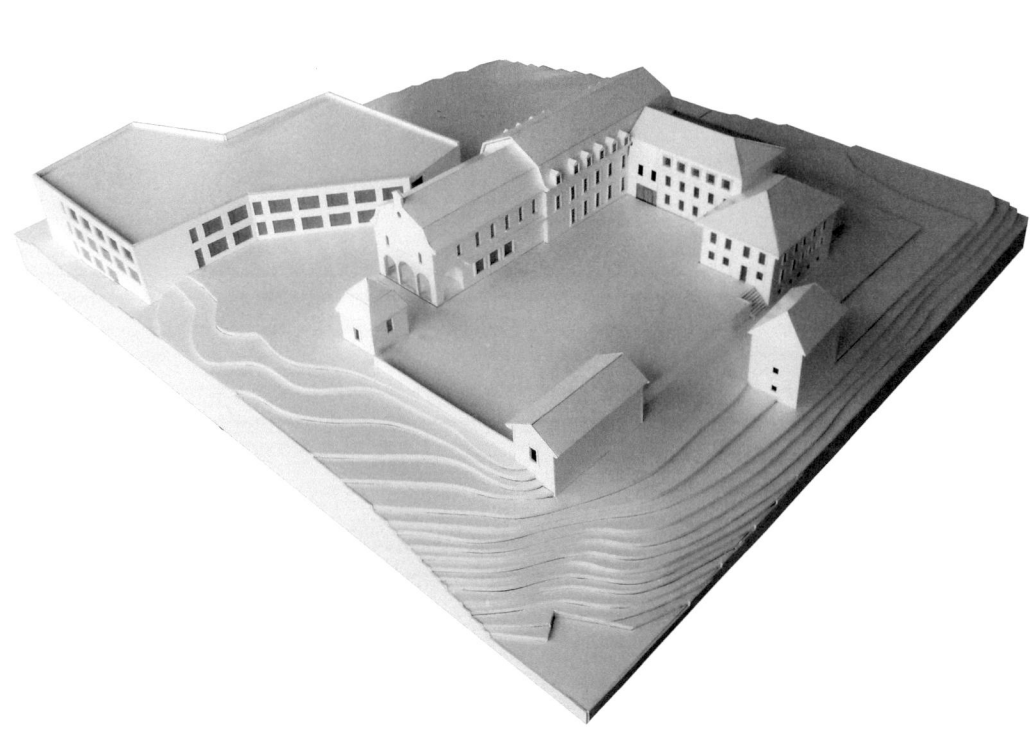

Werkverzeichnis / List of Works
Auswahl Bauten, Projekte und Wettbewerbe / Selection of buildings, projects and competitions

2005		Wettbewerb Gemeindesaal, Cologny; 2. Preis
		Wettbewerb Berufsschule, Freiburg i. Ü.; 5. Preis
		Wettbewerb Collège de Gambach, Freiburg i. Ü.; 2. Preis
2006	1	Villa Duboux, Lutry
		Wettbewerb Verwaltungsgebäude Gruppe E, Freiburg i. Ü.; 6. Preis
2007	2	Arnon-Schule, Fiez (Wettbewerb 2004; 1. Preis)
		Schulzentrum, Vers-chez-les-Blanc (Wettbewerb 2003; 1. Preis)
		Wettbewerb Wohn- und Pflegeheim Plein-soleil, Lausanne; 2. Preis
		Flugzeugwaschhalle, Payerne (Wettbewerb 2004; 1. Preis)
2008		Schulzentrum Léman, Gebäude «Vaudaire», Renens (Wettbewerb 2005; 1. Preis)
		Wettbewerb Wohnquartier Fontenette, Genf; 4. Preis
		Wettbewerb Wohnanlage, Onex; 3. Preis
2009		Schulzentrum Léman, Umbau Gebäude «Joran», Renens (Wettbewerb 2005; 1. Preis)
		Studentenwohnheime, Saint-Sulpice (Wettbewerb 2006; 1. Preis)
		Wettbewerb Studentenwohnheim, Genf; 4. Preis
		Wettbewerb Kindertagesstätte Eve de Pinchat, Genf; 1. Preis
		Wettbewerb Turnhalle, Béthusy; 2. Preis
		Wettbewerb Anlage für betreutes Wohnen, La Charrette; 2. Preis
2010		Umgestaltung der Rue du Bourg, Lutry
		Wettbewerb Mietshaus, Gland; 3. Preis
		Wettbewerb Flugstützpunkt, Payerne; 2. Preis
		Wettbewerb Orientierungsschule, Martigny; 4. Preis
		Wettbewerb Pres-Grange, Corsier; 5. Preis
		Wettbewerb Collège du Platane, Froideville; 2. Preis
		Wettbewerb Erweiterung einer Schule, Vernay; 3. Preis
2011		Wohn- und Pflegeheim Bois-Gentil II, Lausanne (Wettbewerb 2004; 1. Preis)
		Wettbewerb Foyer Petit-Maître, Yverdon; 3. Preis
		Wettbewerb ECA Les Fiches, Lausanne; 4. Preis
		Wettbewerb Badeanlage Montoly, Gland; 4. Preis

1 2 3

2011		Wettbewerb Campus der SUPSI, Lugano; 7. Preis
		Wettbewerb Anlage für betreutes Wohnen, Payerne; 2. Preis
		Wettbewerb Schulkomplex, Bex; 4. Preis
2012		Wettbewerb Wohnanlage Fiches Nord, Lausanne; 4. Preis
		Wettbewerb Öffentliche Einrichtungen Parc Geisendorf, Genf; 4. Preis
		Wettbewerb COEL, Renens; 3. Rang, Erwähnung
2013	3	Umbau Recordon 1, Lausanne (Studienauftrag 2011)
		Wettbewerb Pflegeheim CSSC Sainte-Croix, 2. Preis
2014		Gemeindehaus, Chavannes-des-Bois (Wettbewerb 2010; 1. Preis)
		Wohn- und Pflegeheim Le Marronnier, Lutry (Wettbewerb 2003; 1. Preis)
		Wohn- und Pflegeheim Pré-Fleuri, Lausanne
	4	Wettbewerb Wohnanlage Secteur L, Vernier; 3. Preis
		Wettbewerb Schülerwohnheim und Krippe En Cojonnex, Lausanne; 4. Rang, 2. Erwähnung
		Wettbewerb Collège Les Fiches, Lausanne, 4. Preis
2015		Stadtvilla Chailly, Lausanne
		Censuy-Schule, Renens (Wettbewerb 2011; 1. Preis)
2016	5	Wettbewerb Pflegeheim Les Tines, Nyon; 3. Preis
	6	Wettbewerb Fondation de Serix, Palézieux; 2. Preis
		Wettbewerb Pflegeheim La Colline, Chexbres; 3. Preis
2017		Wettbewerb Pflegeheim Le Christ-Roi, Lens; 2. Preis
		Wettbewerb Fachschule En Guillermaux, Payerne; 1. Preis
		Wettbewerb Wohnungen SCHL, Bussigny; 1. Preis

Laufende Projekte

Wohn- und Pflegeheim Les Fauvettes, Montagny-la-Ville (Wettbewerb 2013; 1. Preis)
Schulzentrum Mabillon, Monthey (Wettbewerb 2011; 1. Preis)
Veranstaltungssaal und Wohnungen, Nyon (Wettbewerb 2012; 1. Preis)
Schulzentrum Léman, Umbau und Erweiterung Turnhalle «Maurabia», Renens (Wettbewerb 2005; 1. Preis)

4
5
6

Alfonso Esposito

1963	geboren in Lausanne
1989	Diplom an der Ecole Polytechnique Fédérale de Lausanne bei Professor Luigi Snozzi
1986	Praktikum im Büro Purini in Rom
1989–1999	Mitarbeiter in den Büros Boschetti und Monod in Lausanne
1993–1998	Assistent der Professoren Paul Chemetov, Yves Lion, Mauro Galantino und Marc Mimram an der EPFL
1999	Gründung des eigenen Büros
2003	Gründung des Büros Esposito & Javet
2000–2005	Präsident der Architektengruppe des waadtländischen SIA
2011–	Mitglied des Bund Schweizer Architekten (BSA/FAS)
2012–2016	Gutachter für Bachelorarbeiten an der Hochschule für Technik und Architektur Freiburg i. Ü.
2013–	Mitglied der Beratungskommission für das Lavaux
1963	Born in Lausanne
1989	Graduated at the Ecole Polytechnique Fédérale de Lausanne under Professor Luigi Snozzi
1986	Training placement at the architectural office Purini, Rome
1989–1999	Employde by the architectural offices of Boschetti and Monod, Lausanne
1993–1998	Assistant to Professors Paul Chemetov, Yves Lion, Mauro Galantino and Marc Mimram at the EPFL
1999	Established own office
2003	Co-Founded own architectural office Esposito & Javet
2000–2005	President of the Vaud Group of the Swiss Society of Engineers and Architects (SIA)
2011–	Member of the Swiss Federation of Architects (FAS/BSA)
2012–2016	Expert for BA reviews at the HEIA Fribourg
2013–	Member of the Lavaux advisory commission

Anne-Catherine Javet

1963	geboren in Genf
1989	Diplom an der Ecole Polytechnique Fédérale de Lausanne bei Professor Luigi Snozzi
1986	Praktikum in den Büros Cruz und Ortiz in Sévilla und Dominguez in Madrid
1989–1997	Mitarbeiterin im Büro Luigi Snozzi in Lausanne
1993–1997	Assistentin von Professor Luigi Snozzi an der EPFL
2003–2004	Assistentin von Professor Luigi Snozzi an der ETH Zürich
1997	Gründung des eigenen Büros
2003	Gründung des Büros Esposito & Javet
2002–2004	Präsidentin des waadtländischen SIA
2006–	Gutachterin für Bachelor- und Masterarbeiten an verschiedenen Hochschulen (EPFL, Hochschulen für Technik und Architektur Freiburg und Genf)
2007–	Mitglied der städtebaulichen Kommission von Lutry
2011–	Mitglied des Bund Schweizer Architekten (BSA/FAS)
2013–	Mitglied der städtebaulichen Kommission von Biel/Bienne
2015–	Mitglied der waadtländischen Architektenkammer
1963	Born in Geneva
1989	Graduated at the Ecole Polytechnique Fédérale de Lausanne under Professor Luigi Snozzi
1986	Training placement at the architectural offices of Cruz and Ortiz, Seville and Dominguez, Madrid
1989–1997	Employed by the architectural office of Luigi Snozzi, Lausanne
1993–1997	Assistant to Professor Luigi Snozzi at the EPFL
2003–2004	Assistant to Professor Luigi Snozzi at the ETH Zurich
1997	Established own office
2003	Co-founded own architectural office Esposito & Javet
2002–2004	President of the Vaud Group of the Swiss Society of Engineers and Architects (SIA)
2006–	Expert for BA and MA reviews in various schools (EPFL, HEIA Fribourg and Geneva)
2007–	Member of the Lutry town planning commission
2011–	Member of the Swiss Federation of Architects (FAS/BSA)
2013–	Member of the Bienne town planning commission
2015–	Member of the Vaud Chamber of Architects

Mitarbeitende / Employees		Tommaso Alberghi, Claudia Awad, Constanze Beer, Christopher Bettex, Irina Blajev, Fabiana Franco, Pascal Jeker, Aladar Kish, Véronique Masset-Emery, Sylwia Strzelczyk, Joana Varela
seit 2003 / since 2003:		Cécile Bertrand, Mikhaïl Broger, Carmen Chabloz, José Garraza, Xaveer Gheysens, Andrew Hugonnet, Michele Lisena, Deirdre McKenna, Gérard Meystre, Anne-Christine Moonen, Marjolaine Obrist, Miguel Pereiro, Albert Pons, Diane de Pourtalès, Ruben Sousa, Claire Thompson, Omar Trinca, Paul Verhoeven, Théo Voegtlin, Fiona Vullo
ehemalige Praktikanten / former trainees:		Pietro Banzato, Marine Bersier, Bertrand Clavel, Elsa Cornu, Andrew Dragesco, Jeanne Garcia, Pilar Gascón Bravo, Noémie Jeunet, Anne Krins, Sarah Lenk, Katharina Littmann, Calum MacDonald, Thierry Manasseh, Nicolas Meyer, Aïda Mitic, Romain Odier, Carlo Piffaretti, Manuel Potterat, Tanja Rodriguez, Vincent Roesti, Claire Rosat, Sandrine Rubin, Marta Ruiz, Gian Serena, Marine Vallois, Mélanie Wills
Paul Chemetov (Textbeitrag / Article)	1928	geboren in Paris
	1959	Diplomabschluss an der l'École Nationale Supérieure des Beaux Arts (Ateliers Lurçat, Vivien, Lagneau Gillet)
	1961–1985	Mitglied des Atelier d'urbanisme et d'architecture (AUA)
	1971–1972	Lehrtätigkeit an der École d'Architecture de Strasbourg
	1978–1989	Lehrtätigkeit an der École Nationale des Ponts-et-Chaussées
	1980	Grand Prix national d'architecture
	1982–1987	Mitglied des Leitungskomitees und später Vizepräsident von Plan Construction
	1993–1994	Gastprofessor an der EPFL
	2007	Gründung des AUA Paul Chemetov
	2009	Präsident des wissenschaftlichen Komitees des Projekts Grand Paris
	2016	Verantwortlicher Leiter der Entwicklungsabteilung der Stratégie Nationale pour l'Architecture (SNA)
		Kommandeur der Ehrenlegion
	2017	Gründung Atelier Masséna (mit Ronald Sirio)
Ausstellungen, Auszeichnungen / Expositions, awards	2010	*Distinction romande d'architecture* (Schulzentrum, Vers-chez-les-Blanc)
	2011	*Best architects 2011* (Schulzentrum Léman, Renens)
		Best architects 2011 (Schulzentrum, Vers-chez-les-Blanc)
		Carte blanche, f'ar – forum d'architectures (Architekturforum), Lausanne
	2016	*Best architects 2016* (Gemeindehaus, Chavannes-des-Bois)
Bibliografie / Bibliography	2004	Wohn- und Pflegeheim Le Marronnier, Lutry. In: Tracés Nr. 21
		Wohn- und Pflegeheim Bois-Gentil II, Lausanne. In: Tracés Nr. 21
	2005	De l'espace dans le volume existant. Histoire d'une rénovation: La Fauvette, Lausanne. In: Habitation Nr. 3
		Gemeindesaal «Le Gerdil», Cologny. In: Tracés Nr. 22
	2007	Neuer Hauptsitz der Groupe E, Granges-Paccot. In: hochparterre.wettbewerbe Nr. 1
		Einfamilienhaus, Lutry, 21 VD. In: 15n SIA Sektion Romandie
		Payerne/VD – Base aérienne. Station de lavage pour avions et véhicules spéciaux. armasuisse immobilier
	2008	Arnon-Schule, Fiez. In: Probatima 03, 2TA-304
		Arnon-Schule, Fiez. In: Lignum Bulletin bois Nr. 89
		Ecole bucolique. Le collège buissonnier de Fiez. In: Bâtir Nr. 9
	2009	Schulzentrum, Vers-chez-les-Blanc. In: Probatima 01, VD-366
		Une coopérative au service des étudiants. In: Habitation Nr. 2
		Einfamilienhaus, Founez, 50 VD. In: 15n SIA Sektionen Romandie und Bern
		Schulzentrum Léman, Renens. Tout en un! In: Chantiers & rénovations Nr. 6
		Didactique de la forme, lecture du lieu. In: Tracés Nr. 21
		Schulzentrum, Vers-chez-les-Blanc. arch 3, service d'architecture de Lausanne
		Nouveau bâtiment de seize classes pour le Collège du Léman. In: Edifice magazine Nr. 6
	2010	Extension scolaire. Jeu subtil entre verre et béton. In: Bâtir Nr. 1
		Extension du Collège du Léman Renens, 38 VD. In: 15n SIA
		Schulzentrum Léman, Renens. In: Architecture & Construction, Ville de Renens, Nr. 1702

2010	Site scolaire du Léman
	Wohn- und Pflegeheim Bois-Gentil II, Lausanne. Etat de Vaud,
	Service de la santé publique
	Schulzentrum, Vers-chez-les-Blanc. In: Distinction romande d'architecture
2011	Schulzentrum, Vers-chez-les-Blanc. In: best architects 11, 69 Projekte
	Schulzentrum Léman, Renens. In: best architects 11, 69 Projekte
	Wohn- und Pflegeheim Bois-Gentil II, Lausanne, VD 30. In: 15n SIA
	Schulzentrum Léman, Renens, Umbau Gebäude «Joran», VD 31. In: 15n SIA
	Arnon-Schule, Fiez. In: en visite… 2006/2011, SIA Sektion Waadt
	Schulzentrum, Vers-chez-les-Blanc. In: en visite… 2006/2011, SIA Sektion Waadt
	«Les estudiantines», Studentenwohnheime, Saint-Sulpice. In: en visite…
	2006/2011, SIA Sektion Waadt
	Erweiterung Schulzentrum Léman, Renens. In: en visite… 2006/2011,
	SIA Sektion Waadt
	EMS Bois-Gentil de 56 lits, un restaurant et une garderie pour 24 enfants,
	Lausanne. In: en visite… 2006/2011, SIA Sektion Waadt
	Chaleureux et accueillant, Bois-Gentil II. In: idea Nr. 6
2013	Ecole supérieure de l'ETML. Etat de Vaud, service immeubles, patrimoine et
	logistique, fiche 102
	Espace et luminosité, Wohn- und Pflegeheim Pré-Fleuri, Lausanne. In: idea Nr. 5
	L'extension tant attendue. Wohn- und Pflegeheim Le Marronnier, Lutry. In: Bâtir Nr. 10
	Collège du Censuy, Renens
2016	Gemeindehaus Chavannes-des-bois. In: best architects 16 award/results
	Collège du Censuy, Renens, VD 46. In: journées SIA
	Gemeindehaus, Chavannes-des-Bois, VD 45. In: journées SIA
	Gemeindehaus, Chavannes-des-Bois. In: A voir 2016 SIA

Finanzielle und ideelle Unterstützung
Financial and conceptual support

Ein besonderer Dank gilt den Institutionen und Sponsorfirmen, deren finanzielle Unterstützungen wesentlich zum Entstehen dieser Buchreihe beitragen. Ihr kulturelles Engagement ermöglicht ein fruchtbares und freundschaftliches Zusammenwirken von Baukultur und Bauwirtschaft.

Special thanks to our sponsors and institutions whose financial support has helped us so much with the production of this series of books. Their cultural commitment is a valuable contribution to fruitful and cordial collaboration between the culture and economics of architecture.

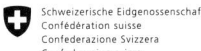

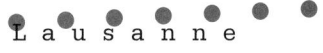

Fondation EMS Le Marronnier, Lutry
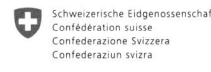

a.planir Sàrl, Echallens

Adani constructions métalliques Sàrl, Crissier

Alberti Ingénieurs SA, Lausanne

Boss & Associés Ingénieurs Conseils SA, Ecublens

Georges Sauteur SA
La Tour-de-Trême

Giacomini & Jolliet
Ingénieurs S.A., Lutry

Perrin & Spaeth, bureau d'ingénieurs conseils SA, Renens

Pierre Chuard Ingénieurs Conseils SA
Le Mont-sur-Lausanne

Regtec SA, Lausanne

Savarioud SA, Misery

Bohren Möbel AG, Baldegg; Bravata SA, Romanel-sur-Lausanne; Félix constructions sa, Denges; Laik SA, Forel; Lambda S.A., Lausanne; Menuiserie Francis Gabriel SA, Chexbres; R. Ottino & Fils Plâtrerie & peinture, Lausanne

Quart Verlag Luzern / Quart Publishers Lucerne

De aedibus – Zeitgenössische Architekten und ihre Bauten / Contemporary architects and their buildings

67	Esposito Javet (de/en und de/fr)	34	Liechti Graf Zumsteg (de/en)
66	Galletti Matter (de/en und de/fr)	33	Adrian Streich (de/en)
65	Fruehauf, Henry & Viladoms (de/en)	32	Daniele Marques (de/en)
64	Jakob Steib (de/en)	31	Neff Neumann (de/en)
63	bunq (de/en)	30	Giraudi Wettstein (de/en)
62	Jean-Paul Jaccaud (de/en und de/fr)	29	Steinmann & Schmid (de/en)
61	huggenbergerfries (de/en)	28	Matthias Ackermann (de/en)
60	Berrel Berrel Kräutler (de/en)	27	Aeby & Perneger (de/en)
59	Pierre-Alain Dupraz (de/en und de/fr)	26	Bakker & Blanc (de/en)
58	Cometti Truffer (de/en)	25	Markus Wespi Jérôme de Meuron (de/en)
57	Joos & Mathys (de/en)	24	Bauart (de/en und de/fr)
56	Lacroix Chessex (de/en)	23	Knapkiewicz & Fickert (de/en)
55	Savioz Fabrizzi (de/en und de/fr)	22	Marcel Ferrier (de/en)
54	Boegli Kramp (de/en)	21	Wild Bär Architekten (de/en)
53	Zita Cotti (de/en)	20	Enzmann + Fischer (de/en)
52	Oestreich + Schmid (de/en)	19	Mierta und Kurt Lazzarini (de/en)
51	Stump & Schibli Architekten (de/en)	18	Rolf Mühlethaler (de/en)
50	Luca Gazzaniga (de/en)	17	Pablo Horváth (de/en)
49	Guignard & Saner (de/en)	16	Brauen + Wälchli (de/en)
48	Morger + Dettli (de/en)	15	E2A Eckert Eckert Architekten (de/en)
47	Charles Pictet (de/en)	14	Lussi + Halter (de/en)
46	Armando Ruinelli + Partner (de/en/it)	13	Philipp Brühwiler (de/en)
45	Luca Selva Architekten (de/en)	12	Scheitlin – Syfrig + Partner (de/en)
44	Luca Deon (de/en)	11	Vittorio Magnago Lampugnani (de/en)
43	2b (de/en)	10	Bonnard Woeffray (de/en und de/fr)
42	Durisch + Nolli (de/en)	9	Graber Pulver (de/en)
41	sabarchitekten (de/en)	8	Burkhalter Sumi / Makiol Wiederkehr (de/en)
40	Beat Rothen (de/en)	7	Gigon/Guyer (de und en)
39	Atelier Bonnet (de/en)	6	Andrea Bassi (de, fr und en)
38	Novaron (de/en)	5	Dieter Jüngling und Andreas Hagmann (de und en)
37	Althammer Hochuli (de/en)	4	Beat Consoni (de und en)
36	Schneider & Schneider (de/en)	3	Max Bosshard & Christoph Luchsinger (de)
35	Frei & Ehrensperger (de und en)	2	Miroslav Šik (de, en und it)
		1	Valentin Bearth & Andrea Deplazes (de, en und it)

Quart Verlag GmbH, Heinz Wirz; Verlag für Architektur und Kunst
Denkmalstrasse 2, CH-6006 Luzern; books@quart.ch, www.quart.ch